The Muslim Educational Trust

Ghu... ...r

...g

...im Bleher

...uhammad Ibrahim

Ibrahim Hewitt

Ruqaiyyah Waris Maqsood

Muhammad Akram Khan-Cheema

Nighat Mirza

Issues in Islamic Education

British Library Cataloguing-in-Publication Data
A catalogue record of this book is available from the British Library

Published by

The Muslim Educational Trust
130 Stroud Green Road
London N4 3RZ
UK
Tel: 0171 272 8502
Fax: 0171 281 3457

ISBN 0 907261 29 9

Printed and bound in Great Britain by

Cromwell Press Limited
Broughton Gifford
Melksham
Wiltshire SN12 8PH
UK
Tel. 01225 782585

Contents

Contributors

SARWAR, Mr Ghulam	*Director, The Muslim Educational Trust, London, UK.*
AD-DARSH, Dr Syed Mitawilli	*President, Islamic Shari'a Council, London, UK.*
SAQEB, Dr Ghulam Nabi	*Visiting Fellow, Institute of Education, University of London, London, UK.*
BUTT, Dr Nasim	*Head of Science, King Fahad Academy, London, UK.*
HUSAIN, (The late) Dr Syed Sajjad	*Former Vice-Chancellor, Rajshahi and Dhaka Universities, Bangladesh.*
BEG, Dr Muhammad Abdul Jabbar	*Former Associate Professor, National University of Malaysia and the University of Brunei Darussalam.*
BLEHER, Mr Sahib Mustaqim	*General Secretary, Islamic Party of Britain, Milton Keynes, UK.*
IBRAHIM, Mr Muhammad	*(Formerly Ian Abrams) Head of Religious Studies, Southgate School, Enfield, London, UK.*
HEWITT, Mr Ibrahim Brian	*Development Officer, Association of Muslim Schools (UK & Eire), Leicester, UK.*
MAQSOOD, Mrs Ruqaiyyah Waris	*(Formerly Rosalyn Kendrick) Head of Religious Studies, William Gee School, Hull, UK.*
KHAN-CHEEMA, Mr M. Akram	*Education Management Consultant, (registered for inspections with the Office for Standards in Education), Bingley, UK.*
MIRZA, Mrs Nighat	*Headteacher, Leeds Muslim Girls School, Leeds, UK.*

In the name of Allāh, the Most Merciful, the Most Kind

Preamble

Read!
in the name of your Lord and Cherisher, Who created;
Created man, out of a (mere) clot of congealed blood:
Read! And your Lord is Most Bountiful,
He Who taught (the use of) the pen,
Taught man that which he knew not.
{Al-Qur'ān, chapter 96, verses 1-5}

Behold! in the creation of the Heavens and the Earth;
in the alternation of the night and the day;
in the sailing of the ships through the ocean for the profit of mankind;
in the rain which Allāh sends down from the skies,
and the life which He gives therewith to an earth that is dead;
in the beasts of all kinds that He scatters through the earth;
in the change of the winds,
and the clouds which they trail like their slaves
between the sky and the earth;
(Here) indeed are Signs for a people that are wise.
{Al-Qur'ān, chapter 2, verse 164}

Verily, this brotherhood of yours is a single brotherhood,
and I am your Lord and Cherisher:
therefore serve Me (and no other).
{Al-Qur'ān, chapter 21, verse 92}

The Muslim Educational Trust would like to thank all the contributors. We pray that *Allāh* rewards them with His choicest blessings for their efforts for His sake. It is hoped that the articles will provoke further in-depth discussion on these and other issues pertaining to Islāmic education.

The views expressed in the articles are those of the authors, and not necessarily those of the Muslim Educational Trust.

Islāmic Education: its meaning, problems and prospects

Ghulam Sarwar

Introduction

The need for an Islāmic education system is not only a matter of conviction, but also crucial for mankind. No other system can save human beings from destruction and perdition, apparent to anyone with insight into and concern for human welfare. On such a system depends the future well-being of all peoples of the world.

Establishing an Islāmic education system in the modern world may seem idealistic, the impractical and unachievable longing of Muslims to revive the Islāmic glory of the period between the seventh and thirteenth centuries. The inherent problems would be both profound and complex, yet despite this we must work towards the establishment of such a system.

The choice is either to survive as human beings with purpose, honour and dignity, or to perish in humiliation and utter despair. The man-made education system has led to many forms of social degeneration: misuse of human intellect and creativity to suit political and economic objectives; abuse of drugs, power, authority and wealth; increased murder and crime; and self-abasement through suicide and euthanasia. The race for the acquisition of nuclear and other weapons, the hoarding and wilful destruction of food (whilst millions starve across the world), discrimination based on race, colour, sex and religion, and attempts to legitimise and even celebrate unnatural acts (sodomy, homosexuality, sado-masochism, etc.) are further instances of our moral decline. Corruption and greed, poverty and lack of basic amenities, and limitations on freedom of expression, even in Muslim countries, make the situation look even bleaker. Wars, genocide, persecution and torture continue even today; whilst the most developed countries supply arms, tacitly supporting abuses of human rights, condemning or acquiescing in an appalling show of double-standards, dictated by political and economic considerations without reference to moral and ethical concerns.

It is clearly logical and desirable to argue for a system based on the Creator's revealed guidance which is the basis for the ultimate success of mankind. The guidance was propagated by divinely inspired messengers in ancient history, and was applied with great success in seventh century Arabia and the adjoining lands of what is now known as the Middle East.

Why did this ideal system not continue? It is the folly of man that he disobeys his omnipotent and omniscient Creator.[1] He has misused the Creator's unique gift of freedom of choice. The tricks and temptations of the Devil *(Iblīs)* – the epitome of arrogance and disobedience[2] – only exacerbate this unfortunate situation. The Creator has given human beings free will to affirm or deny Him, in order to test their faith. Human beings are thus responsible for their actions and will be held to account by the Creator. His gift of freedom of choice is a sign of His munificence and supreme power.

The All-Powerful Creator, in His infinite mercy, sent His final messenger, Muḥammad ﷺ – the last in a chain of about 124,000 prophets (including Adam, Noah, Abraham, Ishmael, Isaac, Moses and Jesus)[3] – as an excellent example[4] for all mankind. The success of mankind depends on voluntary, conscious and complete submission to the Creator, based on this example.

Islām is the best way of life, originating from the transcendent and unique reality, *Allāh* (God) – the Creator. However, many non-Muslims regard it as a restrictive faith promoting rigid laws and patriarchy; they scorn it and its adherents at every opportunity. This may be because of an unwillingness to understand, or because of age-old prejudices dating from the crusades of the eleventh, twelfth and thirteenth centuries, reinforced by daily misrepresentations in the Western media; it may even be due to perceptions of modern Muslim countries. The ignorance, prejudice, misrepresentation and misinterpretation of Islām are unacceptable in a world where information can be obtained in seconds thanks to advances in technology. This prejudice and resulting injustice should be addressed objectively.

The absence of a model Islāmic education system in any Muslim country has added to the problem. Had there been one, it would have served as an example attracting students from all over the world for its excellence in learning, character building and benefit to mankind. For the time being it remains a dream due to the lack of a proper programme of action or the expertise and political will to change, and due to excessive dependence on the Western system. Most importantly, Muslims today are greatly lacking in strong faith in *Allāh*, faith that characterised their predecessors in the seventh century CE. The situation will only change when Muslims realise their mistakes and revive their faith, courage and determination. *Allāh's* blessings, mercy and unlimited favour will help the dream to become a reality when a group of His slaves decides to work towards this. *Allāh* does not change the condition of people until they first change themselves.[5]

Most Muslim countries follow the Western secular education system; Muslim students from all over the world have for many decades been going to modern centres of learning, e.g. Oxford, Cambridge, The Sorbonne, Harvard, etc. This contrasts with Islām's period of glory from the seventh to the thirteenth century, when students from the then known parts of the world used to go to Madīnah, Damascus, Baghdād, Al-Azhar (Cairo), Alexandria, Qairanwān, Tunis, Fez and Qurṭubah (Córdoba) for the best education.

When discussing the introduction of an Islāmic education system, it is important to compare it with the current system, based mainly on:

a) the sovereignty of man and superiority of his reason;
b) knowledge acquired by human reasoning and experience;
c) unlimited freedom of thought and expression;
d) unwillingness to accept anything supernatural;
e) individualism, relativism and materialism.

This system has contributed to man's tremendous progress in science, technology, knowledge and experience. It has enabled man to benefit from many of nature's resources. But though man has learnt to fly the skies, cross rivers and oceans, climb hills and mountains, and travel through space, he has lost himself; his bestiality has overtaken his humanity, beauty and, above all, purpose of existence – faith in the All-Powerful, All-Knowing Creator. Despite its material achievements, the system has produced the terrible scenario mentioned earlier; it has debased human beings.

Attempts to improve the existing system will continue to result in failure, for as long as man does not surrender himself to the unique and transcendent Creator, there will be no escaping the disastrous consequences of disobeying Him.

The only solution is to build on the legacy and achievements of Prophet Muḥammad ﷺ, who demonstrated superbly by his excellent example the efficacy of the Islāmic way of life.

Purpose of Creation of Human Beings

A thoughtful and careful look at everything around us should prove convincingly that the universe, with all its creatures, wonders, splendours and mysteries, has a Creator Who, with His unlimited powers, is immaculately and flawlessly controlling it with a definite purpose.[6] This Creator and Controller is *Allāh*, the All-Knowing, All-Wise and

All-Powerful.[7] He has created the universe and everything in it for the benefit and use of man – the most important of all creatures.[8] The purpose of the creation of human beings is obedience to *Allāh's* commandments and wishes *('Ibādah)*.[9] This obedience aims to ensure peace and well-being in society, without prohibiting use of human intellect and free will which should be applied to fulfil the purpose of creation and to promote human welfare.

Human beings are the agents of *Allāh (Khalīfatullāh)*[10] on the Earth. An agent, by its very nature, has to behave in exact accordance with the wishes of the Creator to fulfil the purpose of its creation. The agent must, therefore, be taught how to achieve this purpose. *Allāh* has taken this responsibility upon Himself and taught His agents about how to conduct their affairs on this Earth. *Ādam*, the first man and a prophet of *Allāh*, and his wife, *Ḥawwā'* (Eve), were blessed with knowledge given by the Creator Himself.[11] We can thus say that education followed man's creation almost immediately. Read *(Iqra')* is the first revealed word in the *Qur'ān*, the final guidance from *Allāh* for mankind. According to a saying of Prophet Muḥammad ﷺ, seeking knowledge is an obligation on every Muslim, male and female. This underlines the crucial importance of education.

Definition and Meaning of Islāmic Education

Islāmic education prepares the agent to carry out successfully his obligations. Without this education, obedience to *Allāh's* commands and acting as a good agent of *Allāh* is impossible.

We can define Islāmic education, then, as the process through which human beings are trained and prepared in a concerted way to do their Creator's bidding in this life *(Dunya)* to be rewarded in the life after death *(Ākhirah)*. It is important to note that the Islāmic view of life is holistic, and rejects any separation between this life, which ends with death, and the eternal life that begins after death. In Islām, mundane, empirical, metaphysical and spiritual matters are interconnected and inseparable. Thus an Islāmic education system prepares human beings for both life on this Earth and the life after death.

Conversely, the present-day education system is, for all practical purposes, based on a materialistic philosophy of life, limited to this life only. It is concerned with the process of preparing children to succeed materially. It deals mainly with mundane affairs, ignoring metaphysical concepts like life after death, Heaven and Hell. In this system, discussion of the accountability of human actions to the Creator Who rewards and punishes with Heaven and Hell, is conducted in an atmosphere of uncertainty, doubt, confusion and lack of objectivity.

> "Education should aim at the balanced growth of the total personality of Man through the training of Man's spirit, intellect, the rational self, feelings and bodily senses. Education should therefore cater for the growth of man in all its aspects: spiritual, intellectual, imaginative, physical, scientific, linguistic, both individually and collectively, and motivate all these aspects towards goodness and the attainment of perfection. The ultimate aim of Muslim Education lies in the realisation of complete submission to *Allāh* on the level of the individual, the community and humanity at large."[12]

"The balanced growth of the total personality of man" cannot be ensured by any system other than the Islāmic education system. The modern secular education system's entire emphasis is on economic growth, the material well-being of the individual and of the society. Children are expected to be prepared, trained and motivated to find their own place in adult life using the skills developed during their education. They are not motivated to pursue the sublime virtues of honesty, decency, truthfulness, justice, fair play, sacrifice, care and concern for the needy and vulnerable, accountability and responsibility. The modern education system hones the worldly instincts of human beings to compete with ferocity in a materialistic world. 'Survival of the fittest' seems to be the norm, despite talk of moral and spiritual development and other finer values of life. Unlimited freedom of inquiry and doubting axiomatic truths are the *sine qua non* of the modern education system. The aim appears to be to produce worldly-wise people uninhibited by principles, rather than decent and responsible human beings with honesty, integrity and a consciousness of the higher values of life. The practice of relativism rather than faith in absolute values has become the trend, epitomised in the 'situation ethics' of the Humanists. This almost all-pervasive relativism has destroyed the basis of higher human values and universalism. Faith in an omniscient Creator, which brings a sense of responsibility, accountability, morality, honesty and decency has become a matter of individual taste and interpretation based on trends and circumstances.

Aim of Islāmic Education

The aim of Islāmic education is to initiate total change in a person – beliefs, actions, potential, faculties, thoughts, expressions, aspirations, energies and everything relating to that person; in other words, the balanced development of the whole personality of a human being – the agent of *Allāh*. It seeks to motivate every member of society to promote and encourage everything good (right) and discourage and forbid evil (wrong). Islāmic education should facilitate the acquisition of knowledge, skills and virtues to achieve success and happiness not only in this life but also in the *Ākhirah*, by the mercy and blessings of *Allāh*. This aim must be known to all involved in education at every level.

Hundreds of thousands of such people – practising Muslims, whose words and deeds were consistent – were inspired by the greatest teacher of mankind, Muḥammad ﷺ, the final messenger of *Allāh*, during his messengership in Arabia between 611-632 CE. These balanced human personalities came both from very humble origins and the highest strata of pre-Islāmic society. They included traders, slaves, labourers, delinquents, adulterers, and leading personalities, both local and foreign, for example: Khadījah bint Khuwailid (555 – 619 CE), Abū Bakr bin Abī Quhafah (d. 634 CE), 'Umar bin Al-Khaṭṭāb (d. 644 CE), 'Uthmān bin 'Affān (d. 656 CE), 'Alī bin Abī Ṭālib (d. 660 CE), Abū 'Ubaidah bin Al-Jarrah (d. 639 CE), Khālid bin Al-Walīd (d. 643 CE), Abū Sufyān bin Ḥarb (d. 652 CE), Bilāl bin Rabāḥ (d. 641 CE), Fāṭimah bint Muḥammad (d. 632 CE), 'Ā'ishah bint Abī Bakr (613 – 678 CE), Khabbāb bin Al-Aratt (d. c. 658 CE), Sumayyah bint Khubbāṭ (d. c. 622 CE), Salmān Al-Fārisi (d. 657 CE), Ḥamzah bin 'Abdil Muṭṭalib (d. 625 CE), 'Abbās bin 'Abdil Muṭṭalib (d. 653 CE) and Usāmah bin Zaid (614 – 674 CE) *(raḍiyallāhu 'anhum)*; some of the early Muslims from a list of many. Such people, by the strength of their faith, brought the Persian and Byzantine empires to heel in the seventh century.

Efforts to Islāmise society should continue simultaneously with efforts to Islāmise knowledge and the introduction of the Islāmic education system. Islāmisation of society cannot be achieved until knowledge is Islāmised on the basis of the *Qur'ān* and the *Sunnah* of the Prophet ﷺ. Only an Islāmised education system can ensure the survival and progress of Islāmic societies. The introduction of an Islāmic education system should be an integral part of the efforts world-wide to establish Islām as an all-encompassing way of life.

Problems of Modern Society

Spiritual and moral issues and development are discussed infrequently in the realm of education, despite social problems such as drug abuse, violence, HIV and AIDS, unmarried mothers, rape, break-up of family life, increase in crime (even vicious attacks on old and vulnerable people by juvenile delinquents, often for only paltry sums of money). Efforts to date have been cosmetic, superficial and ineffective, and cannot be expected to cure deep-rooted problems and produce miraculous results. The solutions to these social problems require acceptance of divine guidance as the basis of our education system. The basic element of the divine guidance *(al-Hidayah)* is a belief that the All-Knowing Creator is the Law-Giver, and that this All-Wise Creator is actively conducting every affair of His Kingdom – the Universe. He guides His worshippers through His prophets and messengers and His revealed Books *(Risālah)*. He is the Guide and He will take a full account from His agents of the affairs of their lives on this Earth on the Day of Judgement *(Yawmuddīn)*. Belief in the *Ākhirah*, where every human being must account for their own actions on this Earth, should bring about a tremendous and revolutionary change in the attitudes and conduct of people, as it did in the past.

It is vital that we mould our education system on these fundamental beliefs (*Tawḥīd*, *Risālah* and *Ākhirah*). This outlook pervades all aspects of our life – social, economic, political, physical, emotional, spiritual, national and international. We should not prolong our predicament by continuing to pursue an almost belief-free and value-free education system. Our education system must be heavily faith-laden and value-laden. No learning is meaningful without a belief in its usefulness and no education is beneficial if it does not transmit and promote deeply cherished values of honesty, integrity, selflessness, concern for social welfare and a strong sense of responsibility and service to others. Though the present education system aims to inculcate these values, such an aim is incompatible with the predominating materialstic outlook on life; thus it cannot be achieved through this system.

Problems in Introducing an Islāmic Education System

The introduction of an education system based on Islām should not be dismissed as the revival of fundamentalism and the curtailment of human freedom of thought and action, nor should it be seen as backward and regressive. The only way forward is to follow consciously and meticulously the way the Creator has ordained for us. He declares in His final book of Guidance (the *Qur'ān*): "Surely the way of life acceptable to *Allāh* is Islām."[13] Contrary to popular Western understanding, Islām did not begin with Muḥammad ﷺ, but began with Ādam, the first man and a prophet of *Allāh*. This system or way is the most enlightened, practised over many millennia by the messengers of *Allāh*, and is the surest method of success. It succeeded for many centuries and must succeed now, *inshā'Allāh* (if *Allāh* wills). It needs determination to work towards this.

The *Qur'ān* exhorts us to prepare ourselves and our children as the 'best of peoples' *(Khair Ummah)* to establish good *(Ma'rūf)* in and to eradicate evil *(Munkar)* from society.[14] This duty is universal and must be acted upon for the benefit of human kind. This aim could be shared by the followers of all religions. Who in their right frame of mind would object to the proliferation of good and the non-proliferation of evil? Everyone, with faith or without faith, should be able to accept this universal message of promoting right and discouraging wrong. Of course, there are varying opinions among people of other faiths, atheists and agnostics about what is right or wrong.

We have been endowed with free will by *Allāh*, and to test us He has created our base desires, instincts[15] and the Devil, and allowed him to try to keep us away from obedience to our Creator. Thus we are beset with baffling, complex problems for which solutions must be found in order to discharge our duty as the agents of *Allāh* on Earth.

The problems that face us in working towards an Islāmic education system are:

a) Unwillingness to accept *Allāh* as the Creator and Guide Whose law is the best and universal.
b) Unwillingness to accept the final messenger of *Allāh* – Muḥammad ﷺ – as the best example (role model) for all mankind.

c) Absence of belief in the metaphysical, e.g. uniqueness of the Creator *(Tawḥīd)*, life after death *(Ākhirah)*, Heaven *(Jannah)* and Hell *(Jahannam)*.
d) Widespread ignorance about the beliefs and teachings of Islām amongst the thinkers and leaders of other faiths and of no faith.
e) Absence of a model to follow in any part of the world, even in Muslim countries.
f) Presence of a bifurcated education system in most Muslim countries; juxtaposition of secular educational institutions and religious institutions.
g) Almost total absence of graded textbooks (revised and corrected to reflect Islāmic beliefs and teachings based on the *Qur'ān* and the *Sunnah*) in all disciplines and fields of human enquiry.
h) Confusing an all-encompassing Islāmic education system with a theological education system which deals only with beliefs, traditions and the moral and spiritual aspects of life, removed from any connection with the needs of the material world.
i) Predominance of philosophies and thoughts not based on the Islāmic view of life and the world (e.g. scholasticism, humanism, materialism, nationalism, positivism, relativism, individualism, scientism, existentialism, etc.).
j) Lack of political will on the part of governments to adopt and implement Islāmic education systems with all its ramifications.

Given the determination, no problem is insurmountable. A beginning has to be made, depending completely on the mercy and blessings of our all-powerful and all-knowing Creator, Who creates anything by a command of one Arabic word *"Kun"* (Be) and it is there.[16] The Creator has created us to work towards the fulfilment of His wishes. He has the power to change and establish anything when He wills to, but He has left it to human beings to bring about the changes.

Present day Muslims seem keen to talk and write about the beauty, superiority and efficacy of Islām, but are noticeably slack in practising it. The need is to practice Islām, complemented by speeches, writings, and conferences, etc. *Allāh* warns us very sternly in the *Qur'ān* about inconsistencies between our words and actions.[17] Our failure to set examples by making our words and actions go together is seriously damaging the image of Islām in the eyes of non-Muslims. This widespread inconsistency is the main reason for the non-recognition of Islām as a practical and viable way of life by non-Muslims, who regard it as a legacy of the past with nothing to offer to the present-day world. We must take a careful look at ourselves and try to remove this impression. As long as we falter in recognising and remedying the inconsistencies between our words and deeds, we will not be taken seriously by any community, especially the materially advanced people of the West. More poignantly, we will be humiliated, marginalised and ignored. This is the state of a billion Muslims all over the world. Unflinching faith in *Tawḥīd*, *Risālah* and *Ākhirah* combined with action *('Amal)* will save us from this humiliation. The need is for voluntary, conscious and complete submission to the Creator's wishes with unwavering faith. Success is then guaranteed by the Creator, Who never fails in His promise.[18]

Doubt or scepticism about these basic concepts, which have been explained by the messengers of *Allāh*, produces disbelief, confusion and uncertainty in man. The sceptics do a great disservice to society, and contribute to social instability and disquiet. They debase the status of man – the *Khalīfah* of *Allāh* on the earth.[19]

The unlettered prophet of Islām, Muḥammad ﷺ, by embodying his words in his deeds, transformed Arab society to bring about a civilisation unequalled before or since, ensuring social welfare. Islāmic history is replete with the wonders brought about by his example. Muslims today are far away from the high standards of faith and action of their great predecessors. Individually and collectively we should build a close and solid bond of love, awe and devotion with our Creator by putting into practice our faith and utterances. All of Allah's messengers embodied their words in their actions; only when we emulate that example will our success be guaranteed.

Basis of Islāmic Education

The purest source of knowledge is the Creator, Who sent down His message for His agents through His selected messengers, by the means of *Waḥi* (Revelation). The archangel *Jibrā'īl* (Gabriel) carried the revelation in its pristine purity to the final messenger of *Allāh*, Muḥammad ﷺ. Angels are special creatures of *Allāh* created from light *(Nūr)*, with no free will; as such can only discharge the function assigned to them without freedom to do otherwise. *Waḥi* is the basis of the highest and surest form of knowledge *('Ilm)*.[20]

Accumulated human experience is a means of gaining knowledge, though such knowledge is neither pure nor always reliable. This empirical knowledge, though essential for education, must be examined carefully in the light of the knowledge received through *Waḥi*.

Any contradiction between knowledge gained through human experience and knowledge based on *Waḥi* must lead us to doubt the reliability of the former. Nevertheless, it could be studied, checked and verified against proven facts. All knowledge should lead man to the achievement of the greater and real purpose of life – *Riḍā'ullāh* by careful compliance with the wishes of the Creator.

Islām encourages freedom of speech and expression, enquiry and thought,[21] but within the limits of responsibility and accountability. No civilisation can prosper if every individual is allowed to misuse and misdirect his *Allāh*-given faculties to proliferate evil, indecency, falsehood or inflammatory ideas causing deep psychological injury to others. *Allāh's* servants should safeguard all decent and wholesome things, including freedom of thought and action within the limits set by the Creator Himself.

Welcome efforts have been and are being made in various parts of the world by some individuals, organisations and Muslim governments to Islāmise the system of education. A concerted attempt to Islāmise the body of knowledge is being conducted under the auspices of the International Institute of Islāmic Thought (IIIT), USA. This effort is particularly laudable, as it is a very basic task without which Islāmisation of education will not be possible. The International Islāmic University of Malaysia has been the main focus of the efforts of the IIIT. Other Islāmic universities, including the Islāmic University in Islāmabad, Pakistan, are also contributing to the Islāmisation of knowledge, but the Islāmic system of education we are discussing still seems to be far from a reality.

Objectives of Islāmic Education

Once *Waḥi*-based knowledge is accepted and acknowledged as the only pure and infallible source of knowledge, and accumulated human experience is regarded as important but fallible and mutable, then the basis of education through which knowledge is imparted is firmly established. The objectives of the Islāmic education system could be summarised as:

1. Prepare and train the future generation to work as agents of *Allāh* on Earth.
2. Ensure the promotion of *Ma'rūf* (good) and the prevention of *Munkar* (evil) in a society.
3. Ensure the balanced growth of the total personality of a person.
4. Promote spiritual, moral, cultural, physical, mental and material development in children in preparation for the responsibilities, experiences and opportunities of adult life.[22]
5. Develop all the faculties to realise the full potential of people.

6. Develop the skills required to enable people to face real-life situations with a clear consciousness about their responsibility and accountability in the *Ākhirah.*
7. Prepare people to work towards the economic and material growth of a society with a strong sense of the unity of the human race and ensure equitable distribution and proper use of wealth.
8. Develop a sense of social responsibility for the efficient use of resources to eliminate wastage, avoid ecological damage, and safeguard the well-being of all created beings.
9. Encourage competition in good things to promote excellence and the highest achievements for the greater welfare of people and society.
10. Ensure that children grow up with a strong belief in sharing opportunities, equity, justice, fair play, love, care, affection, selflessness, honesty, humility, integrity and austerity.

Islāmic education should focus on Islām as the complete system of life, the conclusion of the religion for mankind that began with *Ādam* (the first man and the prophet of the Creator), and culminated with Prophet Muḥammad ﷺ – the final messenger of the Creator for the whole of mankind. Islām, the last of the revealed religions, embodies axiomatic truths of its precursors (e.g. Judaism, Christianity). The Islāmic world-view does not contradict, rather it complements the view held by the other Abrahamic faiths. Islām can be considered to be the convergence point that upholds the truths and beauty of all revealed religions. Islām represents the completion of the favour of *Allāh* for Mankind. The Islāmic way of life is *Allāh's* chosen way.[23]

The Western view of life has been influenced by the thoughts and ideas of philosophers and theologians like Socrates (469 – 399 BC), Plato (428 – 348 BC), Aristotle (384 – 322 BC), St. Augustine of Hippo (354 – 430 CE) and St. Thomas Aquinas (1225 – 1274 CE). The medieval and modern Western thinkers and philosophers include Alighieri Dante (1265 – 1321 CE), Copernicus (1473 – 1543 CE), Francis Bacon (1561 – 1626 CE), René Descartes (1596 – 1650 CE), John Locke (1632 – 1704 CE), Gottfried Wilhelm Leibniz (1646 – 1716 CE), Voltaire (1694 – 1778 CE), Jean-Jacques Rousseau (1712 – 1778 CE), Immanuel Kant (1724 – 1804 CE), Johann Wolfgang von Goethe (1749 – 1832 CE), Georg Wilhelm Friedrich Hegel (1770 – 1831 CE), Auguste Comte (1798 – 1857 CE), John Stuart Mill (1806 – 1873 CE), Charles Darwin (1809 – 1882 CE), Karl Marx (1818 – 1883 CE), Friedrich Nietzsche (1844 – 1900 CE), Sigmund Freud (1856 – 1939 CE), Bertrand Russell (1872 – 1970 CE), Jean-Paul Sartre (1905 – 1980 CE) and others. Most of the modern philosophers and sociologists, including René Descartes and Auguste Comte, accept only modern scientific knowledge as truth, and discard any metaphysical concept not compatible with and experimentable by human senses. Man is considered as just another part of nature. Transcendent reality or anything ontological is not acceptable. This leads to atheism or agnosticism, as it does not recognise or is sceptical about the existence of the Unique, Everlasting, All-Powerful Creator. Western philosophy focuses on individualism (freedom and liberty of individuals to attain the best of what they want). Islām, however, presents a world-view and a life stance based on total submission to the Creator and the welfare of all peoples of the world. This global view of Islām is paramount and should be reflected in its educational philosophy.

Unbridled use of reason and experiments to reach conclusions on matters beyond human intellect should be abandoned in favour of divine guidance. Whilst the tremendous contribution of the West to the development of knowledge should be acknowledged and credited, at the same time its science, technology, philosophy, politics and economics should be reviewed objectively by Muslim scholars to use them selectively and creatively for the benefit of humankind.

Islām upholds the view that the world and the people in it represent a unity both in origin and purpose.[24] Despite their diversity in colour, race, language, religious beliefs and traditions, Islāmic education would emphasise that human beings have a common origin and a common destiny.

An Islāmic education system would recognise the different needs of people living in parts of the world with marked variation in climate and circumstances. The unity of origin and goal would be highlighted by the recognition of diversity of circumstances but not of faith. Faith in the transcendent Creator will remain central and unalterable.

Some Practical Steps in the Introduction of an Islāmic Education System

Having dealt with the basic principles and objectives, and clarified the usefulness and importance of an Islāmic system of education, it is now essential to look at the practical aspects of a whole range of issues involving curriculum, syllabuses, text books and other educational resources, teacher training, meeting the diverse needs of disparate geographical territories, and the feasibility of implementing such a system globally.

A prerequisite to this programme is the recognition of the need for such an education system by the political leadership of a society. Education, in the societal context, is a political initiative. The political leadership should recognise and accept the need both in theory and in its practical implications.

1. **Plan**: A phased plan of action will take into account: goals and targets, time-scale, provision of resources (human and material), monitoring, implementation, and measurement of success.
2. **Infrastructure**: The present systems and procedures, buildings and premises (those with value-free architecture) will be maintained but brought into line to reflect Islām'*s* world-view and its unalterable stance of *Khalīfatullāh* and obedience (*'Ubūdīyah)* to the Creator. Essential changes to infrastructure will be made, namely facilitating the observance of Islāmic duties by the construction of additional mosques and provision of places of worship and other amenities for non-Muslims (in Muslim countries) in educational institutions.
3. **Ending bifurcation**: Most Muslim countries have a dichotomy in the education system between religious and secular educational institutions. The products of modern secular institutions predominate at every level of the materialistic society, whereas those of religious institutions remain outside the mainstream of society, catering only for some religious and spiritual needs. The present religious education system is flawed and falls short of the needs of an age of science and technology. Rather than becoming centres of excellence for both worlds (this world and the next), they have been reduced to an irrelevance in the race for material advancement. It is curious to note that in several Muslim countries Islāmic universities exist separately from secular universities.

   The modern secular system of education and religious seminaries, including the Islāmic universities, would be merged into an integrated system, to make an all-encompassing Islāmic education system.
4. **Curriculum**: All beneficial knowledge not against belief in the Creator will continue to be taught and applied. Existing curricula, syllabuses, text books and teaching resources will be critically examined and revised to reflect the Islāmic view of human beings and the world based on the teachings of the *Qur'ān* and the *Sunnah.* A broad-based curriculum, recognising diversity in location and needs, should be prepared by a team of experts with clarity of purpose, commitment, and complete *Tawakkul* (reliance) on *Allāh* for the success of the project. The curriculum will be based primarily on revealed knowledge and secondarily on acquired knowledge.
5. **Syllabuses**: Detailed syllabuses should be prepared for each subject or area of a

discipline by a team of suitable experts for:

(a) Revealed knowledge – study of the *Qur'ān* (reading, memorisation, understanding, application and hermeneutics); study of the *Sunnah* (collection, transmission, authenticity, categorisation and application, etc.); study of the *Sīrah*; study of Islāmic *Sharī'ah, Fiqh* and *Uṣūl al Fiqh*; study of Qur'ānic Arabic;

(b) Acquired knowledge – Humanities, Linguistics, Social Sciences, Natural Sciences, Medical Sciences, Technology and others.

6. **Text Books**: Text books on subjects and disciplines mentioned in (b) above must be examined by experts in those subjects. Any books whose contents are against the principles of Islām should be revised, discarded or replaced. This is a stupendous task, but an absolute necessity for the successful implementation of the Islāmic education system. The need has already been recognised by some Islāmic educationists and scholars, and appreciable ground work has already been done by, amongst others, the IIIT.

New text books should be written on selected areas of acquired knowledge by scholars of exceptional ability; they should reflect creativity, originality and advancement to faith-laden human knowledge to make Islāmic education a success for all mankind. No task is insurmountable if there is faith in *Allāh*. Believers and those who work for *Allāh's* pleasure are successful.[25] Muslim exegetes, jurists, sociologists, theologians, mathematicians, philosophers and historians have produced great works on areas of revealed knowledge and human enquiry. They include: 'Abdullāh bin Ma'sūd (d. 653 CE), 'Abdullah bin 'Abbās (d. 688 CE), 'Abdullāh bin 'Umar (d. 693 CE), Imām Ja'far Aṣ-Ṣādiq (d. 765 CE), Imām Abu Hanīfa (d. 767 CE), Ibn Isḥāq (d. 767 CE), Imām Abū Yūsuf (d. 795 CE), Imām Mālik (d. 795 CE), Jabir bin Ḥayyān (d. 815 CE), Imām Ash-Shāfi'ī (d. 820 CE), Ibn Hishām (d. 834 CE), Ibn Sa'd (d. 845 CE), Al-Khawārizmī (d. 850 CE), Imām Aḥmad bin Ḥanbal (d. 855 CE), Imām Bukhārī (d. 870), Al-Kindī (d. 870 CE), Imām Muslim (d. 875 CE), Ibn Mājah (d. 886 CE), Abū Dāwūd (d. 888), At-Tirmidhī (d. 892 CE), An-Nasā'ī (d. 915 CE), Ibn Jarir al Tabarī (d. 923 CE), Al-Mas'ūdī (d. 956 CE), Ibn Sinā (Avicenna, d. 1037 CE), Ibn Al-Ḥaithām (Al-Hazen, d. 1040 CE), Al-Birūnī (d. 1051 CE), Ibn Ḥazm (d. 1064 CE), Aṭ-Ṭusī (d. 1067 CE), Imām Ghazālī (d. 1111 CE), Al-Zamakhsharī (1144 CE), Ibn Rushd (Averroes, d. 1198 CE), Ibn Al-Jawzī (d. 1200 CE), Ibn Al-'Arabī (d. 1240 CE), Al-Qurṭubī (d. 1273 CE), Ibn Taimīyah (d. 1328 CE), Ibn Kathīr (d. 1373 CE), Ibn Khaldūn (d. 1406 CE), Jalaluddīn As-Suyuṭī (d. 1505 CE), Shah Walī Allāh (d. 1762 CE), Muḥammad bin 'Abdul Wahhāb (d. 1791 CE), Muḥammad Iqbal (d. 1938 CE), Ḥasan Al-Banna (d. 1949 CE), Sayyid Qutb (d. 1966 CE), Sayyid Abul A'lā Mawdūdī (d. 1979 CE), Ismā'īl Rāji Al-Fārūqī (d. 1986 CE), and many others. Their admirable works should be built on, leading to further research into and the application of revealed knowledge, guiding and directing the course of acquired knowledge, and addressing contemporary issues.

7. **Teacher Training**: The pivotal importance of teachers in Islāmic education must be acknowledged; indeed, all messengers and prophets were essentially teachers. The teacher is the transmitter of knowledge – revealed and unrevealed. He is the embodiment of the message. He represents the practical manifestation of the knowledge contained in the message. *'Ilm* (knowledge) and *'Amal* (practice) must be combined. One without the other is a tree without fruits. The message needs to be applied so its benefits can be appreciated by those for whom it is intended. The *Dīn* (way) of *Allāh (*Islām*)* in its pristine purity has to be established in its totality – so declares the *Qur'ān*, the final revealed book of the Creator.[26] This responsibility has to be accomplished by Islāmic teachers when they transmit

revealed knowledge and empirical knowledge.

The teachers by their superb example of *Taqwā*[27] (piety, or consciousness of *Allāh*) embodying the highest state of faith, *Ihsān*, will motivate and inspire their students to continue the propagation of the message of *Allāh*.

Teachers must be trained by people having *Taqwā* and exemplary knowledge and practice of Islām. Although they may be few and far between, some such people are available. Our duty is to find them and to benefit from them.

8. **Stages of Education**: Every stage of education, e.g. nursery, primary (elementary), secondary, higher (vocational and university) should be planned within an Islāmic system.

   Setting up a few institutions of a certain level in both Muslim and non-Muslim countries (say, nursery, primary or secondary) is undoubtedly a bold step in the right direction, but must be seen in the overall context of the whole education system – its purpose, usefulness and eventual success in preparing children as *Khalīfatullāh* (agents of *Allāh*) in an age of science, technology, competition and excellence. Competition and excellence *per se* must not be seen as ends in themselves, but rather considered within the remit of *Khilāfah* and *Riḍā' ullāh*.

9. **Arabic**: This should be the *lingua franca* of Islāmic education. It is the language of the *Qur'ān*, which contains entirely the words of the transcendent Creator, *Allāh*. It is the main language spoken in over twenty countries, and is used by Muslims across the world, especially in their *Ṣalāh* (obligatory daily prayers). All Muslims should learn to recite, read and understand the *Qur'ān*. The recasting of acquired knowledge on the basis of the *Qur'ān* and the *Sunnah* will be impossible without thorough knowledge of classical and modern Arabic. Teaching Arabic as a language must be an integral part of the curriculum of an Islāmic education system.

10. **Private and State support**: The system, whilst encouraging private initiatives and support, will depend principally on the State. Provision of Islāmic education has to be the main priority of Muslim governments.

11. **Needs of women**: Women constitute over half of the human race, and their needs should be properly looked after, in keeping with their status and role as defined by Islām. They should be able to play their part as the agents of *Allāh* in the society in which they live.

12. **Needs of non-Muslims**: An Islamic education system ought to address the needs of non-Muslims (in Muslim countries); arrangements should be made to meet their special needs.

13. **Muslim minorities**: In countries where Muslims are in a minority, the introduction of an Islāmic education system would be difficult until a suitable model is available. Until a model Islāmic education system comes into existence, the responsibility of providing Islāmic education to children will continue to lie with Muslim parents. The *Qur'ān* exhorts Muslims to save themselves and their families from Hell.[28]

    Muslims in non-Muslim societies are required to act as role models by being living examples of Islām, making a positive impression on the non-Muslim majority as they witness the beauty and efficacy of the Islāmic way of life.[29]

Conclusion

Islāmic education will not merely reform a human being, rather it will bring about his total transformation. The metamorphosis of the individual in Islām will be total and complete. The slave Bilāl and prospective killer 'Umar were transformed into outstanding personalities and heroes par excellence. Perpetrators of horrific acts are less likely to emerge from an Islāmic education system. That could only be possible with the decline of the system. Rather than cosmetic or superficial change, the Islāmic system will ensure the total development of children's personalities so that they grow into shining examples of honesty, integrity, intellect and consistent conduct. The change that will be brought about in an Islāmic system will be self-evident – there would be genuine felicity and happiness in the society.

Islāmic education and a global Islāmic revival are inextricably connected. This revival should not be seen as a threat of a clash between civilisations[30], of 'the next war', a perpetual confrontation[31]; rather, it should be welcomed as the basis of co-existence, understanding and greater human welfare and success. We should approach the twenty-first century with a message of hope, understanding, cooperation and co-existence rather than Islāmophobia based on misunderstanding, ignorance and prejudice. The memories of the crusades, fanaticism and bigotry should be laid to rest but not forgotten and a new beginning made. Rather than unfairly branding Islām and Muslims as intolerant and terrorists, an era of understanding and peaceful co-existence should begin, ensuring justice and happiness for all the people of the world. Islāmic education should be the precursor of this universal revival based on belief in the uniqueness of the Creator, His universal final message for mankind sent through His final messenger Muḥammad ﷺ, and the certainty of our death and life after death. All human beings have a common origin, a common purpose, and a common Creator – *Allāh* (God).[32]

Muslims, numbering over a billion across the world, owe it to themselves and to the rest of mankind to demonstrate convincingly that the Islāmic education system is the only way forward for all the people of the world. I hope that with total reliance on *Allāh* and faith in His mercy and blessings, efforts to establish the Islāmic system of education for the benefit of all mankind will, *inshā'Allāh*, lead to real success. I further hope that this humble treatise will motivate others with similar thoughts to work towards the achievement of this noble goal.

Success can only come from *Allāh*.[33] Indeed *Allāh* loves those who put their trust in Him.[34] And our duty is only to deliver the clear message.[35]

References

1. Nay, but man doth transgress all bounds, in that he looketh upon himself as self-sufficient.
   (Al-Qur'ān, chapter 96, verses 6-7)

2. … "Bow down to Ādam" and they bowed down.
   Not so Iblīs: he refused and was haughty. He was of those who reject Faith.
   (Al-Qur'ān, chapter 2, verse 34)

   … Not so Iblīs; he refused to be of those who bow down.
   (Al-Qur'ān, chapter 7, verse 11)

   … He said, "Shall I bow down to one whom Thou didst create from clay?"
   (Al-Qur'ān, chapter 17, verse 61)

   … They bowed down except Iblīs.
   He was one of the Jinns, and he broke the Command of his Lord.
   (Al-Qur'ān, chapter 18, verse 50)

3. To every people (was sent) a messenger …
   (Al-Qur'ān, chapter 10, verse 47)

   … But thou art truly a warner, and to every people a guide.
   (Al-Qur'ān, chapter 13, verse 7)

   For We assuredly sent amongst every People a messenger,
   (with the Command), "Serve *Allāh*, and eschew Evil." …
   (Al-Qur'ān, chapter 16, verse 36)

4. We sent thee not, but as a Mercy for all creatures.
   (Al-Qur'ān, chapter 21, verse 107)

   Ye have indeed in the messenger of *Allāh* an excellent exemplar (of conduct) …
   (Al-Qur'ān, chapter 33, verse 21)

And surely you have the excellent (tremendous) morals.
(Al-Qur'ān, chapter 68, verse 4)

5. ... Verily never will *Allāh* change the condition of a people
until they change it themselves (with their own souls) ...
(Al-Qur'ān, chapter 13, verse 11)

6. Behold! in the creation of the Heavens and the Earth;
in the alternation of the night and the day;
in the sailing of the ships through the ocean for the profit of mankind;
in the rain which *Allāh* sends down from the skies,
and the life which He gives therewith to an earth that is dead;
in the beasts of all kinds that He scatters through the earth;
in the change of the winds,
and the clouds which they trail like their slaves between the sky and the earth;
(Here) indeed are Signs for a people that are wise.
(Al-Qur'ān, chapter 2, verse 164)

It is He Who maketh the stars (as beacons) for you, that ye may guide yourselves, with their help, through the dark spaces of land and sea. We detail Our signs for people who know.

It is He Who hath produced you from a single person:
here is a place of sojourn and a place of departure.
We detail Our signs for people who understand.

It is He Who sendeth down rain from the skies:
with it We produce vegetation of all kinds:
from some We produce green (crops), out of which We produce grain, heaped up (at harvest);
out of the date-palm and its sheaths (or spathes) (come) clusters of dates hanging low and near:
and (then there are) gardens of grapes, and olives, and pomegranates,
each similar (in kind) yet different (in variety):
when they begin to bear fruit, feast your eyes with the fruit and the ripeness thereof.
Behold! in these things there are signs for people who believe.
(Al-Qur'ān, chapter 6, verses 97-99)

Not for (idle) sport did We create the Heavens and the Earth and all that is between!
(Al-Qur'ān, chapter 21, verse 16)

Blessed is He Who made constellations in the skies,
and placed therein a Lamp and a Moon giving light;

And it is He Who made the night and the day to follow each other:
for such as have the will to celebrate His praises or to show their gratitude.
(Al-Qur'ān, chapter 25, verses 61-62)

We created not the Heavens and the Earth and all between them merely in (idle) sport.
We created them not except for just ends, but most of them do not know.
(Al-Qur'ān, chapter 44, verse 38)

Blessed be He in Whose hands is Dominion; and He over all things hath Power.

He Who created Death and Life, that He may try which of you is best in deed:
and He is the Exalted in Might, Oft-Forgiving.

He Who created the seven heavens one above another.
No want of proportion wilt thou see in the Creation of *(Allāh)* Most Gracious.
So turn thy vision again: seest thou any flaw?
(Al-Qur'ān, chapter 67, verses 1-3)

7. *Allāh!* There is no god but He, the Living, the Self-subsisting, Eternal.
No slumber can seize Him nor sleep.
His are all things in the Heavens and on Earth.
Who is there can intercede in His presence except as He permitteth?
He knoweth what (appeareth to His creatures as) before or after or behind them.
Nor shall they compass aught of His knowledge except as He willeth.
His Throne doth extend over the Heavens and the Earth,
and He feeleth no fatigue in guarding and preserving them;
for He is the Most High, the Supreme (in glory).
(Al-Qur'ān, chapter 2, verse 255)

8. Do ye not see that *Allāh* has subjected to your (use) all things in the Heavens and on Earth,
and has made his bounties flow to you in exceeding measure, (both) seen and unseen? ...
(Al-Qur'ān, chapter 31, verse 20)

And He has subjected to you, as from Him, all that is in the Heavens and on Earth.
Behold, in that are Signs indeed for those who reflect.
(Al-Qur'ān, chapter 45, verse 13)

9. **I have only created Jinns and men, that they may serve Me.**
(Al-Qur'ān, chapter 51, verse 56)

10. Behold, thy Lord said to the angels: "I will create a vicegerent on earth." ...
(Al-Qur'ān, chapter 2, verse 30)

11. And He taught Ādam the nature of all things; ...
(Al-Qur'ān, chapter 2, verse 31)

Then learnt Ādam from his Lord words of inspiration, and his Lord turned towards him;
for He is Oft-Returning, Most Merciful.
(Al-Qur'ān, chapter 2, verse 37)

12. From the Recommendations of the First World Conference on Muslim Education, Makkah, 1977.

13. **The Religion before *Allāh* is Islām (submission to His Will) ...**
(Al-Qur'ān, chapter 3, verse 19)

... **This day have I perfected your religion for you, completed My favour upon you,
and have chosen for you Islām as your religion** ...
(Al-Qur'ān, chapter 5, verse 4)

14. Ye are the best of peoples, evolved for mankind,
enjoining what is right, forbidding what is wrong, and believing in *Allāh* ...
(Al-Qur'ān, chapter 3, verse 110)

15. "Yet I do not absolve my own self (of blame):
the (human) soul certainly incites evil ...
(Al-Qur'ān, chapter 12, verse 53)

"Did I not enjoin on you, O ye children of Ādam, that ye should not worship Satan;
for that he was to you an enemy avowed?"
(Al-Qur'ān, chapter 36, verse 60)

From the mischief of the whisperer (of Evil) who withdraws (after his whisper),
who whispers into the hearts of Mankind.
(Al-Qur'ān, chapter 114, verses 4-5)

16. To Him is due the primal origin of the Heavens and the Earth.
When He decreeth a matter,
He saith to it: "Be," and it is.
(Al-Qur'ān, chapter 2, verse 117)

... When He hath decreed a plan, He but saith to it, 'Be,' and it is!"
(Al-Qur'ān, chapter 3, verse 47)

For to anything which We have willed, We but say the word, 'Be', and it is.
(Al-Qur'ān, chapter 16, verse 40)

... When He determines a matter, He only says to it, 'Be', and it is.
(Al-Qur'ān, chapter 19, verse 35)

Verily, when He intends a thing, His Command is, 'be', and it is!
(Al-Qur'ān, chapter 36, verse 82)

... It is He Who gives Life and Death;
and when He decides upon an affair, He says to it, 'Be', and it is.
(Al-Qur'ān, chapter 40, verse 68)

17. Do ye enjoin right conduct on the people, and forget (To practise it) yourselves,
and yet ye study the Scripture? Will ye not understand?
(Al-Qur'ān, chapter 2, verse 44)

O ye who believe! Why say ye that which ye do not?

Grievously hateful is it in the sight of *Allāh* that ye say that which ye do not.
(Al-Qur'ān, chapter 61, verses 2-3)

18. So lose not heart, nor fall into despair; for ye must gain mastery if ye are true in faith.
(Al-Qur'ān, chapter 3, verse 139)

"Our Lord! Grant us what Thou didst promise unto us through Thine apostles,
and save us from shame on the Day of Judgement. For Thou never breakest Thy promise."
(Al-Qur'ān, chapter 3, verse 194)

... To those who do good, there is good in this world,
and the Home of the Hereafter is even better, and excellent indeed is the Home of the righteous.
(Al-Qur'ān, chapter 16, verse 30)

... "Fear ye not!" (they suggest),
"Nor grieve! but receive the Glad Tidings of the Garden (of Bliss), the which ye were promised!"
(Al-Qur'ān, chapter 41, verse 30)

19. **Many are the Jinns and men we have made for Hell:**
They have hearts wherewith they understand not,
eyes wherewith they see not, and ears wherewith they hear not.
They are like cattle – nay more misguided: for they are heedless (of warning).
(Al-Qur'ān, chapter 7, verse 179)

We have indeed created man in the best of moulds.

Then do We abase him (to be) the lowest of the low.
(Al-Qur'ān, chapter 95, verse 4-5)

20. Say: "I am but a man like yourselves,
(but) the **inspiration *(waḥi)*** has come to me, that your *Allāh* is one *Allāh*:
whoever expects to meet his Lord, let him work righteousness,
and, in the worship of his Lord, admit no one as partner.
(Al-Qur'ān, chapter 18, verse 110)

Say thou: "I am but a man like you.
It is revealed to me by **inspiration *(waḥi)***, that your *Allāh* is one *Allāh*:
so stand true to Him, and ask for His Forgiveness."
And woe to those who join gods with *Allāh*.
(Al-Qur'ān, chapter 41, verse 6)

It is no less than inspiration sent down to him:

He was taught by one Mighty in Power,

Endued with Wisdom: for he appeared (in stately form);

While he was in the highest part of the horizon:

Then he approached and came closer,

And was at a distance of but two bow-lengths or (even) nearer;

So did *(Allāh)* convey the inspiration to His Servant – (conveyed) what He (meant) to convey.
(Al-Qur'ān, chapter 4, verse 10)

(Allāh) Most Gracious!

It is He Who has taught the *Qur'ān*.

He has created man:

He has taught him speech (and intelligence).
(Al-Qur'ān, chapter 55, verse 1-4)

21. Behold! in the creation of the Heavens and the Earth;
in the alternation of the night and the day;
in the sailing of the ships through the ocean for the profit of mankind;
in the rain which *Allāh* sends down from the skies,
and the life which He gives therewith to an earth that is dead;
in the beasts of all kinds that He scatters through the earth;
in the change of the winds,
and the clouds which they trail like their slaves between the sky and the earth;
(Here) indeed are Signs for a people that are wise.
(Al-Qur'ān, chapter 2, verse 164)

Behold! Abraham said: "My Lord! Show me how Thou givest life to the dead."
He said: "Dost thou not then believe?"
He said: "Yea! but to satisfy My own undertaking.."
He said: "Take four birds; tame them to turn to thee;
put a portion of them on every hill and call to them: they will come to thee (Flying) with speed.
Then know that *Allāh* is Exalted in Power, Wise."
(Al-Qur'ān, chapter 2, verse 260)

Behold! in the creation of the Heavens and the Earth, and the alternation of night and day,
there are indeed signs for men of understanding.
(Al-Qur'ān, chapter 3, verse 190)

"It is those who believe and confuse not their beliefs with wrong
that are (truly) in security, for they are on (right) guidance."

That was the reasoning about Us, which We gave to Abraham (to use) against his people.
We raise whom We will, degree after degree; for thy Lord is full of wisdom and knowledge.
(Al-Qur'ān, chapter 6, verses 82-83)

It is He Who maketh the stars (as beacons) for you, that ye may guide yourselves, with their help,
through the dark spaces of land and sea. We detail Our signs for people who know.

It is He Who hath produced you from a single person;
here is a place of sojourn and a place of departure.
We detail Our signs for people who understand.

It is He Who sendeth down rain from the skies;
with it We produce vegetation of all kinds;
from some We produce green (crops), out of which We produce grain, heaped up (at harvest);
out of the date-palm and its sheaths (or spathes) (come) clusters of dates hanging low and near:
and (then there are) gardens of grapes, and olives, and pomegranates,
each similar (in kind) yet different (in variety);
when they begin to bear fruit, feast your eyes with the fruit and the ripeness thereof.
Behold! in these things there are signs for people who believe.
(Al-Qur'ān, chapter 6, verses 97-99)

Verily, in the alternation of the night and the day,
and in all that *Allāh* hath created, in the Heavens and the Earth,
are signs for those who fear Him.
(Al-Qur'ān, chapter 10, verse 6)

Say: "Travel through the Earth and see how *Allāh* did originate creation;
so will *Allāh* produce a later creation: for *Allāh* has power over all things.
(Al-Qur'ān, chapter 29, verse 20)

Seest thou not that the ships sail through the ocean by the Grace of *Allāh*,
that He may show you of His signs?
Verily in this are signs for all who constantly persevere and give thanks.
(Al-Qur'ān, chapter 31, verse 31)

Glory to *Allāh*, Who created in pairs all things that the earth produces,
as well as their own (human) kind and (other) things of which they have no knowledge.

And a sign for them is the night:
We withdraw therefrom the day, and behold they are plunged in darkness;

And the Sun runs his course for a period determined for him:
that is the decree of (Him), the Exalted in Might, the All-Knowing.

And the Moon, We have measured for her mansions (to traverse)
till she returns like the old (and withered) lower part of a date-stalk.

It is not permitted to the Sun to catch up the Moon, nor can the night outstrip the day:
Each (just) swims along in (its own) orbit (according to Law).

And a sign for them is that We bore their race (through the Flood) in the loaded Ark;

And We have created for them similar (vessels) on which they ride.
(Al-Qur'ān, chapter 36, verses 36-42)

22. cf. The Education Reform Act 1988, UK, sec. 1 (2)(a)(b).

23. ... **This day have I perfected your religion for you,
completed My favour upon you,
and have chosen for you Islām as your religion** ...
(Al-Qur'ān, chapter 5, verse 4)

24. **Verily, this Brotherhood of yours in a single Brotherhood
and I am your Lord and Cherisher, therefore serve me (and no other).**
(Al-Qur'ān, chapter 21, verse 92)

And verily this Brotherhood of yours is a single Brotherhood,
and I am your Lord and Cherisher, therefore fear Me (and no other).
(Al-Qur'ān, chapter 23, verse 52)

25. So lose not heart, nor fall into despair; for ye must gain mastery if ye are true in faith.
(Al-Qur'ān, chapter 3, verse 139)

... It is the party of *Allāh* that must certainly triumph.

(Al-Qur'ān, chapter 5, verse 59)

The believers must (eventually) win through.
(Al-Qur'ān, chapter 23, verse 1)

Already has Our Word been passed before (this) to Our servants sent (by Us),

That they would certainly be assisted,

And that Our forces – they surely must conquer.
(Al-Qur'ān, chapter 37, verse 171-173)

26. It is He Who hath sent His Messenger with guidance and the Religion of Truth, to cause it to prevail it over all religion, even though the Pagans may detest (it).
(Al-Qur'ān, chapter 9, verse 33)

It is He Who has sent His Messenger with Guidance and the Religion of Truth, to cause it to prevail over all religion: and enough is *Allāh* for a Witness.
(Al-Qur'ān, chapter 48, verse 28)

It is He Who has sent His Messenger with Guidance and the Religion of Truth, that He may make it prevail over all religion, even though the Pagans may detest (it).
(Al-Qur'ān, chapter 61, verse 9)

27. O mankind! We created you from a single (pair) of a male and a female,
and made you into nations and tribes,
that ye may know each other (not that ye may despise (each other).
Verily the most honoured of you in the sight of *Allāh* is (he who is) the most righteous of you.
And *Allāh* has full knowledge and is well acquainted (with all things).
(Al-Qur'ān, chapter 49, verse 13)

28. **O ye who believe!**
save yourselves and your families from a Fire whose fuel is Men and Stones ...
(Al-Qur'ān, chapter 66, verse 6)

29. Thus, have We made of you an *Ummah* justly balanced,
that ye might be witnesses over the nations, and the Messenger a witness over yourselves; ...
(Al-Qur'ān, chapter 2, verse 143)

Let there arise out of you a band of people
inviting to all that is good,
enjoining what is right,
and forbidding what is wrong.
They are the ones to attain felicity.
(Al-Qur'ān, chapter 3, verse 104)

30. Samuel P. Huntington, 'The Clash of Civilisations', *Foreign Affairs*, Summer 1993, vol. 72, no. 3, pp. 22-49.

31. Brian Beedham, 'Islām and the West (survey)', *The Economist*, 6 August 1994, vol. 332, no. 7875.

32. **Say: "O People of the Book! Come to common terms as between us and you:**
That we worship none but *Allāh*; that we associate no partners with him;
that we erect not, from among ourselves, Lords and patrons other than *Allāh*."
If then they turn back, say ye:
"Bear witness that we (at least) are Muslims (bowing to *Allāh's* Will)."
(Al-Qur'ān, chapter 3, verse 64)

And verily this Brotherhood of yours is a single Brotherhood,
and I am your Lord and Cherisher: therefore fear Me (and no other).
(Al-Qur'ān, chapter 23, verse 52)

33. ... and my success (in my task) can only come from *Allāh*.
In Him I trust, and unto Him I look."
(Al-Qur'ān, chapter 11, verse 88)

34. ... Then, when thou hast taken a decision put thy trust in *Allāh*.
For Allāh loves those who put their trust (in Him).
(Al-Qur'ān, chapter 3, verse 159)

35. "And our duty is only to deliver the clear Message."
(Al-Qur'ān, chapter 36, verse 17)

Note: The Qur'ānic references are based on 'Abdullāh Yūsuf 'Alī's translation, revised and edited by the Presidency of Islāmic Researches, Ifta, Call and Guidance, Riyadh, Saudi Arabia.

Islām and the Education of Muslim Women

Dr S. M. Ad-Darsh

Al-Islām is the final way of life bestowed on mankind by revelation from *Allāh (subḥānahu wa taʻalā)*. The revelation is preserved in two basic sources: the *Qur'ān* – the pure, eternal word of *Allāh*, and the *Sunnah* – the explanation of the *Qur'ān* by the final messenger of *Allāh*, Muḥammad ﷺ through his words, deeds and his approval of the deeds of others. *Allāh* has endowed His word with the quality that no one has the power to tamper with it. As He said in His Book (the *Qur'ān*),

> *We have, without doubt, sent down the Message;*
> *And We will assuredly guard it (from corruption).*[1]

The same, to a certain degree, is true of the *Sunnah* of the Prophet.

Universality of the Message

One of the basic attributes of *Allāh* is that He is the Most Compassionate. His compassion, as the Creator of the universe, is to be extended to all of His creation. That was one reason why, when the Prophet was preaching in the tiny town of Makkah, with just a few converts around him, the *Qur'ān* stressed that its mission and message was not confined to Makkah alone, or the Arabian peninsula or the Arabic-speaking communities elsewhere. Rather, it was for all human beings:

> *We have not sent you but as a universal Messenger to men*
> *giving them glad tidings and warning them.*[2]

> *Blessed is He, Who sent down the Criterion to His servants*
> *that it may be an admonition to all creatures.*[3]

The Nature of Religion

From an Islāmic perspective, religion is not a personal matter to be confined to the area of the God-man relationship; of course, this is the core of all the revealed religions but it cannot function properly if limited to such a narrow area. Man is created with two important elements - the physical and the spiritual.

> *Behold, Your Lord said to the angels,*
> *"I am about to create man from a sounding clay,*
> *from mud moulded into shape.*
> *When I have fashioned him (in due proportion)*
> *and breathed into him from My spirit,*
> *fall you down in obedience to him."*[4]

These two basic components of man need to be satisfied in a proportionate manner to prevent one from starving the other or denying it its due consideration. That means religion has to be comprehensive in nature to cater for the spiritual as well as the physical needs of man. If this proposition were true for the earlier, periodic messages from *Allāh*, then it is even more relevant for a message which is going to remain the moulding factor for humankind until the end of this earthly life.

The Two Sections of Humanity

If a religion represents the real force of change in human society, it cannot, rationally speaking, address itself solely to one section, the male of the species, leaving out of its jurisdiction the more influential section, the female. Society may be able to limp along on one leg, but it cannot move forward steadily and successfully without the other leg. Or, put another way, there is an Arabic proverb which says, "A single hand cannot clap."

The concept of the creation in Islām is one of a partnership of two equal parties with varying functions. In chapter four of the *Qur'ān*, *Allāh* says,

> *O mankind! Reverence your Guardian Lord,*
> *Who created you from a single person,*
> *created of like nature his mate*
> *and from them twain scattered (like seeds)*
> *countless men and women.*[5]

Every time *Allāh* states in the *Qur'ān* 'O you who believe!' or 'O mankind!', He is calling the attention of both men and women. One Qur'ānic verse mentions no less than ten good basic characters in both the masculine and feminine sense:

> *"Surely the men who submit and the women who submit,*
> *and the believing men and the believing women,*
> *and the devout men and the devout women,*
> *and the truthful men and the truthful women,*
> *and the patient men and the patient women,*
> *and the humble men and the humble women,*
> *and the charitable men and the charitable women,*
> *and the fasting men and the fasting women,*
> *and the men who guard their chastity*
> *and the women who guard their chastity*
> *and the men who remember Allāh much*
> *and the women who remember Allāh much,*
> *Allāh has prepared for them forgiveness and a mighty reward."*[6]

From a theoretical point of view, in Islām, what is good for men is, generally, good for women. There are few exceptions to this maxim. However, such exceptions deal with the nature and function of the female rather than reflect badly upon her competence morally or rationally.

The Formative Period

This outlook of Islām was the reason for the great moral, social and financial eminence exhibited during the golden era of Islām. Men and women were the recipients of the guidance of *Allāh* and His revelation at the hands of the Prophet, peace be upon him. He was entrusted by *Allāh* to teach people the Book and Wisdom and this the Prophet did to both male and female. The sister of 'Umar was, by the Grace of *Allāh*, responsible for his acceptance of the faith; Sumayyah, the wife of Yāsir (the father of 'Ammār) was the first martyr in Islām.

After the establishment of the faith and the teaching of the Islāmic way of life with full strength, women were present in the mosque of the Prophet along with the men. When it became difficult for women to gain a private audience with the Prophet they complained to him; he directed the women to chose a suitable day upon which he could meet them regularly. "Some women requested the Prophet to fix a day for them as the men were taking all his time. On that he promised them one day for instruction."[7] It is also recorded that the Prophet gave the good news that "if a man had a slave girl and educated her in the best possible way, then gave her her freedom and married her, he will be rewarded twice."[8]

Muslims are aware of the great contribution of the Mother of the Faithful, 'Ā'ishah to the spread of Islāmic knowledge. She is considered to be among the great seven *muftis* of the companions. Umm Salama, another Mother of the Faithful, is considered to be one of the thirteen *muftis* after the premier seven. She is classed amongst Abū Bakr, Abū Hurairah and 'Uthmān. Allama Al-Gilāni, in his explanation of *al-Adab al-Mufrad* (The Unique Manner) by Al-Bukhārī, said that Abul Walīd At-Tayalisi, one of the great traditionists, reported *aḥādīth* from no less than seventy female *muḥaddithah*. This was at the beginning of the 3rd century after the *Hijrah*.

One of the nice stories about the great Hanafi scholar Al-Kasāni, nicknamed 'The King of the Scholars', was that he married Fāṭimah, daughter of As-Samarqandi, the teacher of Al-Kasāni. Fāṭimah was a great pupil of her father and used to sign *fatwas* alongside him. Showing admiration for his bright pupil, As-Samarqandi gave his daughter to Al-Kasāni. Afterwards, *fatwas* would be signed by all three of them. When her husband was mistaken, Fāṭimah would correct him. If he was called the 'King of the Scholars', then she, as of right, deserves to be their Queen!

Reaction

However, not very long after the great reform of the social and cultural position of women in Islāmic society had begun, a reaction against this trend arose.

There are two traditions, of different authorities, said to be attributed to the Prophet ﷺ through 'Ā'ishah and Ibn 'Abbās; the wording of both is nearly the same. The great *muḥaddith* Shaikh Shamsul Ḥaqq al-Azimabadi wrote an article dealing with the question of teaching women to read and write. He affirmed the permissibility of that but before reaching this conclusion he had to deal with the said statements of the Prophet related by the Mother of the Faithful and Ibn 'Abbās. The alleged statements read: "Do not accommodate your women in the upper floors, nor teach them reading and writing. Teach them how to spin and the chapter of The Light *(Al-Nūr)*." (allegedly related by 'Ā'ishah) And, "Do not teach them (women) writing. Do not accommodate them in the upper rooms (or places). The best amusement of the woman is the spindle and the best amusement of the man is swimming." Other versions are nearly the same.

The great *muḥaddith* Shaikh Abadi, true to his profession, traced the line of all such narrations, those who narrated them and what had been extensively said about them and came to the conclusion that they are false statements which have no basis whatsoever. Nevertheless, this has not prevented many eminent scholars of *tafsir* from quoting such statements. What does this reflect? It reflects a deep-rooted bias against women. 'Ā'ishah, the intelligent, adept and witty scholar – who is supposed to be a supporter of women's rights – is reported to have said: "If the Prophet had witnessed what women invented, he would have stopped them coming to the mosque!" This notion was strongly opposed by Ibn Ḥazm who said, "If we accept such an argument, everyone would say, 'If the Prophet had seen this, if the Prophet had seen that' and the rules of *Sharī'ah* would be eroded one after the other. *Allāh* Most High knew what women were going to do, but He did not tell His Messenger to stop them going to the mosque."

Shaikh Abadi mentioned the sound hadith in which a clear request on the part of the Prophet was made to a female companion to teach Ḥafṣah, daughter of 'Umar, and his wife how to use a charm. In Abū Dāwūd's *Sunan* it is recorded that Ash-Shafa, daughter of 'Abd Allāh, said, "The Prophet ﷺ entered Ḥafṣah's place while I was there. He said, 'Will you not teach her how to use the ant charm, as you taught her how to write?'" The ant is a sort of boil which appears on the side of the body which causes the sensation of an ant walking and biting the skin.

After a thorough investigation of those who reported the *ḥadīth*, Muslim scholars came to the conclusion that it is sound and it can be taken as a basis for the permissibility of teaching women to read and write.

The reason I have had to deal at some length with the statements 'prohibiting' such teaching is to dispel the baseless notion that Islām forbids the education of girls. Once this point is clear, what remains is the basic Islāmic attitude towards knowledge, represented in the first revelation speaking about the value of knowledge and the many Qur'ānic verses to the same effect. As far as ahadith are concerned, it is enough to remember that in every manual of *hadīth*, there is a section known as 'The Book of Knowledge' dealing extensively with knowledge in its widest sense.

Again we have to remember that in the area of knowledge there is no discrimination between male and female. The well-established *hadīth*, "Seeking knowledge is incumbent upon every Muslim" is much clearer in its English translation, there being no gender involved; in Arabic it is in the male gender, although Muslim scholars say that "...upon every Muslim" includes the females too. From a juristic point of view, the male gender in such a sentence construction includes the female because both are addressed by *Sharī'ah* injunctions.

A Case of Necessity

It is a well-established rule that Muslim society is under a collective obligation – *Farḍ Kifayah* – to have enough professional personnel to cater for the needs of the society. Muslim jurists say that there has to be enough tailors, bakers, teachers, *Imāms*, judges, medical people and midwives, etc. to satisfy the needs of the community. Muslims prefer female doctors for examining females, males to examine males. From a professional point of view this is much better. From a religious point of view it is essential. Unless, therefore, we have females in such professions we will be failing in our religious duty.

Selective Education

Questions about the Islāmic attitude towards educating Muslim girls may appear to be irrelevant at this time; even the most 'rigid' regimes are educating their girls, with the advancement of technology making it easy for those wealthy enough to buy the best in education for their daughters.

However, the question of selectivity has never been more relevant than it is today because Muslims are following, in the words of the Prophet, "the ways of the people before you, step after step. Even if they entered into a narrow hole you are going to enter it." The obsession of 'education for all is affecting our systems of education and we now see our universities graduating miners, car repairers and painters.

For the future happiness and stability of the Muslim family, the question of selectivity is an essential question which has to be dealt with from a practical, as well as a decency, point of view. As Muslims we should not lose sight of the basic duty of a Muslim woman. She is a mother first, and only then does her profession or whatever come into the picture. Her success will be measured by her success in bringing up stable, integral, happy and morally-sound generations. Any achievement in addition to that is a bonus. You cannot claim a bonus when you haven't had your basic 'wage'.

"And Allāh says the truth and guides to the right way."

1. *Al-Qur'ān*, chapter 15, verse 9.
2. *Ibid.*, chapter 34, verse 28.
3. *Ibid.*, chapter 25, verse 1.
4. *Ibid.*, chapter 15, verses 28-29.
5. *Ibid.*, chapter 4, verse 1.
6. *Ibid.*, chapter 33, verse 35.
7. *Ṣaḥīḥ Al-Bukhārī* , The Book of *'Ilm* (Knowledge).
8. *Ṣaḥīḥ Al-Bukhārī.*

Teacher Training in Islām: its importance and practicalities

Dr Ghulam Nabi Saqeb

Introduction

"Valueless is the Muslim who is not a student or a teacher" (Ḥadīth)

The above pronouncement of a value judgement comes from a man who himself never attended a school and never became literate. When he was forty, he was honoured, while meditating at night, with the visitation of a celestial being, the archangel Jibrā'īl (Gabriel) who, with an overpowering authority from Almighty *Allāh*, commanded him to read. Overawed with this unexpected and impossible demand the man, Muḥammad ﷺ, managed only to mutter, "What shall I read? I cannot read." Three times Jibrā'īl overwhelmed him and pressed his body hard to infuse into his breast the majesty and light that was the Divine Word and then encouraged him again to read. And, lo, Muḥammad found himself reciting what Jibrā'īl read out to him. Thus began the revelation to Muḥammad of the Divine Guidance, the Book, *Al-Qur'ān*, and Muḥammad was chosen to be the prophet of *Allāh*. The two embodiments of *Allāh's* commandment, the Divine Logos and its recipient, the Prophet, then became the ideal archetypes for Islāmic education. In the process of comprehending and complying with the Divine Will, and following the Prophet, the Muslims then evolved a magnificent Islāmic civilisation and a universalistic culture.

Civilisations predating that have left legacies of splendid cultures, towering achievements and lofty monuments but the hallmark of the Islāmic civilisation must remain its uncompromising commitment to monotheism, its insistence on primacy of the revealed knowledge and its success in involving people from all sections and classes of society in the pursuit of learning and gaining of social distinction. By using the power of Divine Knowledge, Islām liberated mankind from the shackles of ignorance and subservience at a crucial period in world history. Feudalism everywhere had nearly crushed the human spirit, restricting access to knowledge to a selected few who were then required to render the benefits of their knowledge to serve their feudal masters and to enslave their fellow human beings. Islām brought knowledge within the reach of all and sundry and exalted those who acquired and practised it higher in rank than even the rulers, so that in the Islāmic domains it was the prince who stood respectfully in front of the scholar instead of the reverse, as was practised in previous civilisations.

Ideal types of teachers

Civilisations are raised and preserved by teachers. Every civilisation defines for itself the image of its ideal teacher whom the young are instructed to emulate. The ancient Greeks, for example, had traditionally regarded poets to be their ideal teachers. But Plato attacked poetry as a misleading and unreliable source of knowledge. Instead, he held the philosopher as a model for his citizens' education and character training.

> "Through the study of dialectic, knowledge of ethics and metaphysics, the philosopher is able", argued Plato, "to concoct suitable myths which instil in the young the qualities of self-control and obedience to their rulers."

Later, another Greek philosopher, Isocrates, proposed the figure of a rhetor to be the ideal teacher whose command over the techniques of style and diction enabled him to prepare his students to state their case in the democratic institutions of Athens.[2]

For the Romans, education meant the faithful preservation and transmission of ancestral mores and virtues which were codified into laws as the Twelve Tables. These laws idealised 'pater familias' or the father as head of the family, to be the ideal teacher. A father's duties towards the education of his son were described in Table Four. He had the authority to imprison, scourge, sell and even slay an offending son. He was responsible for initiating his son into the traditions of Rome and for teaching him all that he would require to pursue his vocation and participate in the business of the state. When, under Greek influence, the Roman schools subsequently became differentiated into elementary and grammar schools, the 'grammaticus' or rhetor was stipulated as the ideal teacher.[3]

The classical Chinese ideal of a teacher was derived from the great sage K'ung Fu Tse (Confucius). The deep-rooted feudalistic traditions of China restricted education to the princely class, the 'lords' who were believed to have perfect minds and perfect characters. The commoners were excluded. The lords had to be trained to emulate the 'grand master', to cultivate traditional wisdom and practise the traditional etiquette, codes and rules of conduct. They were not to be imparted any technical skill for they were not required to engage in any job.[4]

The ancient Hindu society was also strictly hierarchical and education was based on the caste system. Only the top priestly caste of Brahmans were to acquire intellectual and spiritual knowledge. The Kashatriyah caste of warriors and administrators were trained in the skills of warfare while the workers, or Vaishas, acquired from their families service skills; but the vast majority of people, the Sudras, or menials, were considered unworthy of education. The highest ideal in education was search for the Divine and the Guru teacher trained the Brahman boys in 'mantras' or rules of religion. Similarly, the Buddhist monks trained novices in their custody into lifelong disciplines and rituals considered necessary for their journey to nirvana.

The Prophet Teacher

It was in the tradition of the revealed religions, Judaism, Christianity and others, before Islām, that monotheism became the central principle of belief and the prophet the ideal teacher. Education was the means of building the Kingdom of God on Earth and the priest or the rabbi became the agent of the church. Both religions have, for centuries, in their own conception of their respective missions, attempted to disseminate the teachings of their prophets Moses and Jesus (peace be upon them). In the Holy *Qur'ān Allāh* has described the educational role of the prophet thus:

> *We sent not an apostle*
> *except (to teach) in the language of his (own) people*
> *in order to make things clear to them.*
> *Now Allāh leaves straying those whom He pleases*
> *and guides whom He pleases.*
> *And He is Exalted in Power, full of Wisdom.*[5]

> *We send the apostles only to give good news*
> *and to warn:*
> *so those who believe and mend (their ways),*
> *upon them shall be no fear,*
> *nor shall they grieve.*[6]

As is manifest in these verses, the prophet teacher had a comprehensive programme of God-centred education for the welfare of man in this world and the next. Prophets have been sent by *Allāh* throughout history and to all nations and tribes to raise peoples' gaze from narrow, immediate and selfish pursuits to universal ideals. They have the responsibility to translate *Allāh's* revelation into programmes of action leading man to a life of eternal peace and harmony. They implement codes of law and morality to civilise people. This is the true meaning of the worship of *Allāh*. Whereas the previous prophets had been sent to a certain people or tribe, the final Prophet of *Allāh*, Muḥammad ﷺ was sent to be the ideal teacher for all mankind. About him, *Allāh* says in the Holy *Qur'ān*:

We have truly sent thee as a witness,
a bringer of glad tidings and a warner...[7]

We have sent thee (O Muhammad)
but as a universal teacher to all mankind,
to give glad tidings and warn (mankind) against sin.
But most men understand not.[8]

First Muslim teachers

Prophet Muḥammad ﷺ immediately set about teaching his people the principles of Islām soon after receiving Divine revelation in Makkah in the year 610 CE. The first teachers of Islām were trained by the Prophet himself through the *Qur'ān* which revolutionised their lives. Above all, he trained them to love and obey *Allāh* and to live righteous lives. He disciplined them and taught them to invite people to *Allāh's* message in a good manner and with wisdom. The first Muslim teachers began to teach new Muslims how to read and recite the verses of the *Qur'ān*. It is recorded that there were only seventeen literate Muslims in Makkah at that time and most of the teaching took place orally. As their demand grew, Muslims teachers began to teach in different localities and tribes in and around Makkah. When a delegation of the tribes of 'Aws and Khazrāj from Yathrib (later known as Madīnah) came to meet the Prophet and accept Islām, they asked him to send a teacher who could teach the new Muslims the fundamentals of Islām.

During the reigns of *Al-Khulafā' Ur-Rāshidūn* (the Rightly-guided Caliphs), 632-661 CE, when the Islāmic domain expanded to all adjoining regions and the need for teachers of Islām increased sharply, *Qur'ān* readers were despatched from Madīnah. The second *Khalīfah*, 'Umar, sent his special officers 'Abdullāh bin Ma'sūd and Abū Mūsā Al-Ashāri to Kūfah and al-Baṣrah respectively to organise the teaching of Islām in these regions. Large central mosques were built in these and other provincial cities and *Ḥalaqas* of scholars began teaching and training teachers.

Muslim teachers in the Golden Age

Throughout the Umayyad *Khilāfah* (661-750 CE) and early parts of the Abbasid *Khilāfah* (750-1258 CE), the training of teachers was carried out in *Ḥalaqah* (circle) schools. Later, in 815 CE, the Abbasids established their celebrated academy, the *Bait al-Ḥikmah* (the House of Wisdom), in Baghdād where the teaching of secular sciences began to be carried out and researched. By this time, educational activity had proliferated all over the Islāmic world and *maktabs* for elementary and preparatory schooling had been set up in increasing numbers. These were within the mosques for mainly Islāmic subjects and outside, in special places such as bookshops, salons and scholars' homes for other subjects. Large numbers of Greek, Syriac, Christian and Jewish teachers were available for teaching in these schools. Meanwhile, in Egypt, the Ismailis established the celebrated Al-Azhar University where they also began to train teachers in an organised manner. However, great impetus was given to the training of teachers of all levels when the famous *Madrasah al-Nizamiyyah* was opened in Baghdād in 1055 CE as the model Islāmic university for the Sunni parts of the Islāmic world. It was there that the learned scholars of Islām undertook to organise a systematic teaching and training programme for teachers from all parts of the Muslim world.[9]

Training of Muslim teachers

Education then was a life-long commitment and students continued to study until they mastered knowledge in all Islāmic sciences and then specialised in a certain field. They were then issued with a *Shahādah* (certificate) which enabled them to teach in any school or college. Students travelled widely in search of renowned teachers in their particular subject and gained access to the most excellent standards of teaching. They were free to teach anywhere as the curriculum was uniform throughout the Islāmic world .

The most common methodology of teacher-training consisted of an initial thorough education of the trainees in all available sciences at graduation and master levels, followed by qualified status conferred at different stages depending on the level they were to teach. In the later stages trainees were required to teach the younger groups in the presence of members of the community and supervised by their own teachers who acted as their mentors and guardians not only for their academic performance but also for their moral character and piety.[10]

Mass education and status of teachers

As mass education spread far and wide, three levels and categories of teachers emerged, namely: elementary teachers for maktabs; tutors for the children of the elite and princely classes; teachers of advanced studies and scholarship at the *madrasahs*. Although the social status and respectability of teachers on the whole was held high, there are anecdotes which indicate that the post of elementary school *(kuttab)* teacher was not considered high in esteem. This is because the economic position of residents in big cities such as Baghdād, Damascus, Cairo, Basra, Isfahan, etc. had improved while the ordinary kuttab teacher was not paid highly. It is also said that the traditions of criticism and caricaturing of teachers had come from Greek literature which was freely available to the educated gentry in Muslim cities. However, as Aḥmad Shalaby has argued, this view should not be taken to apply to the teaching profession as a whole as there were teachers of unequalled knowledge and piety who commanded the greatest respect and prestige in society.[11]

Teachers who acted as tutors to the sons of the *Khulafā'* and the ruling classes were held in high esteem and rewarded handsomely by the families as well as the students when they, in turn, came to power. Most *Khulafā'* and nobility, when appointing a tutor for their sons, gave specific instructions as to the main qualities expected of both of them. A typical set of instructions is reproduced here:

> "I will reward you, sir, as well as I can for the task for which I have chosen you. Receive him (my son) with a frown and a smile. Teach him to sit with gravity and to stand erect. Do not bore him with long lessons but do not grant him too much leisure should he ask for it. Accustom him to perform his religious duties and teach him to perform the ablutions thoroughly... Teach him the Book of *Allāh* for it is the strong rope and do not let him forget it for that is a dead loss..."[12]

Status of master scholars

The history of Islāmic education is full of records which throw light on the prestige and honour in which learned scholars were held. It is said of many scholars that when they passed through the street men stood in rows to salute them and kiss their hands. Men would often dismount to stand and walk in front of the great teachers out of respect. It is also recorded that not only was this respect shown to the learned scholars by Muslims but also by Christian and Jewish citizens. A certain Abbasid *Khalīfah* was asked if, having reached the highest position in the world, he would still covet any other position. He replied that there was one position that surpassed all that he had acquired and to the status of which there was no equal; it was to sit in a learned man's place to teach people and enrich them. Similarly, it is recorded that once *Khalīfah* Hārūn al-Rashīd happened to be visiting the town of Rakkah when the population had invited a great contemporary scholar to a public meeting. Such was the size of the crowd gathered to pay homage to the scholar that Hārūn's freed slave, who watched the scene, exclaimed "People are forced to come out to receive the *Khalīfah*, but to greet the *Shaikh* they come out in great numbers of their own free will!"[13]

Clearly, such honour was shown to Muslim teachers because they followed in the footsteps of the ideal teacher, the Prophet of Islām. They were devoted to the cause of Islām and were pious and upright. They acted as the guardians of the faith and public good. They saw their role, in those days of monarchic rule, as being to promote good and to ward off evil and they stood firm in defence of Islām, safeguarding the rights of their people. That is why good Muslim rulers took pride in hosting scholars and sought their advice, whereas despotic rulers dreaded them. It was indeed due, in the main, to the quality and character of the Muslim teachers that those centuries became known as the glorious prime of the Islāmic civilisation. Teaching was considered to be the most noble calling and an act of *'Ibādah* (worship). This is why a typical Muslim teacher spent his days in the classroom, lecture hall, library or laboratory and his nights on the prayer mat seeking guidance and strength from *Allāh*.

Decline of scholarship and the teacher

With the passage of time, Islāmic scholarship began to stagnate and decline. Just as the rulers became indifferent in their duty to promote education and scholarship, so did scholars lose their zeal for research and innovation in the pursuit of knowledge. Islāmic education then became repetitive and a faithful preservation and following of the well-trodden path. To be sure, *madrasahs* and *maktabs* continued to function for a long time, financed as they were from the income derived from large scale *waqf* funds which had come down through the ages and still remained in force. However, it was more *taqlīd* (traditionalism) than originality and innovation which characterised their curricula and methodologies. The teacher and the scholar then began to seek nominal recognition and unearned rewards by writing panegyrical poems for the rulers instead of deserved recognition for achievements in the advancement of learning.

A case in point is the well-know censure delivered by the last great Mughal emperor, Muḥīuddīn Aurangzeb, to his own tutor when, after the emperor's crowning, the latter came to pay homage in the hope of obtaining some high reward:

> "Pray, what is your pleasure with me, Mullahji," exclaimed the emperor. "Do you pretend that I ought to exalt you to the first honours of the state? Let us examine your title to any mark of distinction. Show me a well-educated youth and I will say that it is doubtful who has the stronger claim to his gratitude, his father or his tutor. But what was the knowledge that I derived under your tuition? You taught me that the whole of Farangistan (Europe) was no more than some inconsiderable island, of which the most powerful monarch was formerly the king of Portugal, then of Holland and afterwards the king of England... you taught me that they resembled our petty rajas, and that the potentates of Hindustan (India) eclipsed the glory of all other kings. What an admirable geographer and how well read a

historian you have proved yourself to be.

"Was it not incumbent upon my preceptor to make me acquainted with the distinguishing features of every nation of the earth; its resources and strength, its modes of welfare, its manners, religion and form of government, and wherein its interests principally consist; and by a regular course of historical reading to render me familiar with the origin of states, their progress and decline; the events, accidents or errors owing to which such great changes and mighty revolutions have been effected?

"You caused me to devote the most valuable years of my life to your favourite hypotheses or systems and when I left you I could boast of no greater attainment in the sciences than the use of many obscure and uncouth terms, calculated to discourage, confound and appal a youth of the most masculine understanding."[14]

Little did Emperor Aurangzeb know, when he was meting out this diatribe to his teacher, that his empire was soon to crumble and the Europeans were already making inroads within his domain. Did he not realise the superiority of the European discipline, knowledge and technology? It did not take very long for the great Mughal empire rule in India to fall before a European trading corporation, the East India Company; and within the span of a hundred years the whole sub-continent found itself glittering as a jewel in the British crown. But it was not merely the collapse of just one Muslim empire, it was the beginning of a far greater defeat and humiliation of the entire Muslim world at the hands of the expanding European colonial powers. For better or worse, the Muslims of the sub-continent were to endure more than two hundred years of colonial rule thanks to the stagnation of their education and the backwardness of Muslim teachers. It was, essentially, a defeat of the latter.

Colonialism, diarchy and the Muslim teacher

The colonial rulers had, naturally, no love for Muslim education and no desire to resuscitate the Muslim teacher. On the contrary, in order to launch their colonial system of education they had first to liquidate the entire antiquated Muslim education system. They dismissed Muslim teachers and forfeited their *waqf* incomes because their expertise and linguistic and pedagogic skills were of no use. Modern Western education was introduced, not to help uphold the traditional Islāmic culture, but to enable Muslims to obtain white-collar jobs in the new administration. The new educational system was introduced to run parallel to and in competition with the old which had already lost its vigour. Thus a diarchy of education appeared whereby the teachers of Islām were to be maintained by the charitable funds of the impoverished Muslim communities while the modern secular teacher was trained at governmental institutions which operated to promote rudiments of European culture and languages. The two rival classes of Muslim teachers carried unequal status, remuneration and opportunities of employment. A trained Muslim teacher of English or French with a few years' education and training had more opportunities of employment, received a better salary and enjoyed higher status than a teacher of Islām with more years of education and a deeper insight into the Islāmic culture and religion. The latter was often made a target of ridicule and abuse and yet, it was he who still chose to follow the 'ideal teacher' and to serve Islām and Muslims, even under adverse conditions. What makes it frustrating for the Islāmic teachers today is the fact that even after independence from the colonial rule the diarchy still exists in most Muslim countries where their status still remains low.

However, it must also be stressed that the colonial period may not be remembered solely for its failings and in purely negative terms. The role of the colonial period in the modernisation of education and culture in the Islāmic world must also be appreciated. In teacher training, for example, it was during this period that Muslim teachers began, for the first time, to be educated in modern theories and practices of effective teaching through pedagogic research. For the first time, educational psychology with its concepts of child development, heredity, environment, nature and nurture; discipline, reward and punishment; methodologies of teaching such as lesson planning, illustrations and pictorial representation of facts and figures; and the use of teaching aids, school visits, data collection techniques, surveys and interviews and extra-curricular activities, sports, social clubs, scouting etc. that had never been known in teacher training programmes in the traditional Muslim education system became essential parts of the modern education in Muslim countries. Teacher training had now become a science instead of the antiquated and pedantic methods of the traditional Muslim education.

Muslim teachers in Britain

A great deal has changed in the field of education in Britain since the 1950s and 60s when the majority of Muslims from different Commonwealth countries came to live and work in this country. At that time, few thought that they would make Britain their permanent home. Only later, when their families came to join them, did they find themselves faced with the problem of the education of their children. At their local, maintained schools, Muslim children received compulsory general education for the statutory period (between the ages of 5 and 16) and their religious education in the supplementary evening and weekend mosque school. Thus, in the school, they were under the influence of the non-Muslim teachers who were trained in the educational traditions of the country, and, in the mosque school they were taught by the *Imām*, who was not a trained teacher but was experienced in the teaching of Islamic studies. Both differed enormously in their background, training, approaches and attitudes. The non-Muslim teacher, with professional commitment, did his best – in spite of his inexperience of multifaith education and in spite of entrenched racism in society – to make the Muslim children feel at home and learn basic skills. The *Imām*, with no teacher training and with his understanding of and affinity with the community, and with the conventional wisdom he had so acquired, nurtured them into Islāmic values and culture. Between such diverse influences, the Muslim children began to develop conflicts of values.

A whole generation of young Muslims have now grown up with this educational background and suffered from its disadvantages. How do they now consider the question of an integrated and balanced education for their own children? How do they propose to prepare the new Muslim teachers who would have a better education and more appropriate professional training to be able to deliver to their children the best general and Islāmic education? How committed are they to join the teaching profession and so to fulfil the dictates of the Prophet's teaching mentioned earlier, if they are to love and follow him ? These are difficult but apt questions to be posed to the second generation of Muslims in this country upon whom now falls the responsibility of promoting the Islāmic educational traditions which their parents managed to uphold under most difficult circumstances they had to face. It is on their commitment towards the Islāmic education in this country that the progress and welfare of the future generation of Muslims here will depend.

It is estimated that there are 250,000 to 400,000 Muslim children receiving education up to university level in Britain and yet the number of Muslim teachers in the country may be less than one thousands. Indeed, the number of trained Muslim teachers of religious education could be less than a dozen in the whole country! The common professional trend among the young seems to suggest that teaching ranks as the lowest in their order of career aspirations. More financially lucrative professions, like accountancy, law, business studies and medicine attract them most. However, slowly this trend seems to be changing. Recent evidence shows that some qualified accountants and other commercial and business professionals are turning to teaching, mainly for its association with people – children, parents and the community – and the challenges it offers. Hopefully, this message will not be lost to the Muslim youth because the need for trained Muslim teachers in all disciplines (and especially for religious education) has never been greater than in today's Britain and tomorrow's Europe.

Opportunities for Muslim teachers

The Education Reform Act, 1988 (ERA) has opened up new challenges and opportunities for the evolution of an appropriate education for the British child of the next century. Basic rethinking of the aims and objectives of teaching in various subject areas, as well as the restructuring of curricula and syllabi, the stipulation of achievement targets at various levels and methodologies of teaching are very much on the agenda of educationalists all over the country. For the first time it has become a statutory duty for county schools with Muslim pupils to include the teaching of Islām in their RE programmes. Religious educationists are earnestly engaged in attempts to devise Agreed Syllabuses that fulfil the requirements of the ERA and to reflect the multifaith nature of British society; to cater for the religious and spiritual education of children of all faiths. As the largest non-Christian religious minority in Britain, Muslims have a duty to take part in this effort; *Allāh* enjoins upon them the duty of co-operating in acts of goodness and piety and avoiding wrong-doing and immorality. There seems to be a prospect, through schools, for the creation of better understanding and toleration among the younger generation of future citizens. The need for trained Muslim teachers has suddenly grown more than ever before. This task can not be fulfilled by the Imāms and adequate number of Muslim teachers of religious education will have to be trained. To this end, the University of Birmingham has introduced a four-year programme of education and training at its Westhill College leading to the award of a B.Ed. degree with special reference to the teaching of Islāmic studies. Other universities and training colleges may also initiate similar programmes. This means that, for the first time in this country, opportunities for the training of Muslim teachers and for Muslim participation in the educational services have arisen. It is therefore their responsibility to contribute to the educational, moral and spiritual progress not only of their own young but also of the future generation of the country as a whole.

The following concerns and considerations about the future of the Islāmic faith and Muslims in Britain and Europe warrant priority action on the part of the Muslim community in this country to invest special efforts and resources to prepare large numbers of Muslim teachers, educators and educational scholars:

1. The questions of religious education and promotion of moral and spiritual welfare of the young through education, which always ranked high on Muslim demands in education in this country, have now been given due importance by their inclusion in the law – Education Reform Act 1988 and subsequent laws. There are, however, areas within these laws where Islāmic values and Muslim cultural norms have either been ignored or marginalised. These areas include: (a) statutory compulsion on the predominance of Christianity in school worship and RE syllabuses; (b) insignificant position given to Muslims on the Standing Advisory Councils on Religious Education (SACREs) despite the fact that Islām constitutes the largest non-Christian minority faith in this country; (c) Islāmic reservations over the contents, methods and objectives of sex education as delivered in schools; (d) specific Muslim children's needs and Islāmic constraints, e.g. Islāmic objections

to nudity among students in showers, in swimming and physical education, dance, drama and art lessons; the Islāmic requirements in dress and uniforms and wearing of head-cover *(ḥijāb)* by Muslim girls; (e) dilemmas faced by Muslim parents over their right to withdraw their children from RE and collective worship and sex education; anti-Islāmic bias and distortion of the Islāmic faith, culture and history in textbooks, reference books and reading materials that persists despite the presence of Muslims in Europe.

All these questions are matters of serious concern for Muslim parents, the majority of whom are either unaware of their rights or unable to deal with them effectively. Therefore, unless there are sufficient numbers of trained Muslim teachers at all levels and of various specialisations, there is no hope that these questions will be properly understood and satisfactorily tackled.

2. The sheer numbers of Muslim students at schools (estimated as up to 400,000) – in some areas there are over 80 per cent Muslim pupils in schools – warrant a far greater representation of Muslim teachers in the teaching profession, especially to teach subjects like RE and to lead school worship and address school assemblies.
3. The continuing refusal of the Government to grant state funding to Muslim schools by approving them as Voluntary-Aided and Grant Maintained schools requires more Muslim teachers to bring about greater awareness among communities in this country over this glaring discriminatory policy so as to mobilise democratic action.
4. But above all, more qualified and trained Muslim teachers and scholars are required in this country and in Europe in order to present to their peoples, in its true form, the truth of Islām which has, for historical and political reasons, been misrepresented and continues to be stereotyped. Just as in the early history of Islām, it is the duty of Muslim teachers to work hard to remove ignorance and prejudice against Islām by their peaceful, rational and wise manner of discourse and dialogue. People in Britain are by and large mature and open to reason. Therefore, they should be approached by well-read and experienced teachers who are trained in *da'wah* work. Again, as Britain has now virtually become the 'University of the World' where peoples from all over the world flock to gain knowledge, Muslim teachers and scholars must become a part of this great 'university' by training themselves in English and other European languages, to disseminate the knowledge of Islāmic concepts, culture and value systems.

To conclude, it is clear that the first part of Prophet Muḥammad's ﷺ above pronouncement has been fulfilled for the Muslims of Britain, under the law of compulsory education by which every Muslim is, by law, either a student or an ex-student. However, the law cannot force Muslims to enter the teaching profession; it is up to the Muslims themselves to comply with the second part of the Prophet's teaching. To follow in the foot steps of the ideal teacher, the Prophet, Muslim young men and women ought to educate themselves in all disciplines in order to enter into all levels of professional life and to prepare themselves as teachers to teach the principles of Islām to the community at large and to influence the moral spiritual growth of the young.

References

1. Shalaby, Ahmad (1954 CE), *History of Muslim Education*, Dar-al-Kashshaf, Beirut, p 162.
2. Holmes, Brian (1963 CE), 'Teacher Education in a Changing World' in *The Yearbook of Education*, pp 41-58.
3. Howie, George (1963 CE), 'Teachers in Classical Greece and Rome' in *The Yearbook of Education*, pp 41-58.
4. Richardson, Thomas (1963 CE), 'The Classical Chinese Teacher' in *The Yearbook of Education*, pp 26-40.

5. *Al-Qur'ān*, chapter 14, verse 4.
6. *Ibid.*, chapter 6, verse 48.
7. *Ibid.*, chapter 33, verses 45.
8. *Ibid.*, chapter 34, verse 28.
9. Shalaby, Aḥmad, op. cit., pp 59-65.
10. Tritton, A.S. (1957 CE), *Materials on Muslim Education in the Middle Ages*, pp 27-46. Also Shalaby, pp 115-140.
11. Munir-ud-din Aḥmed (1968 CE), *Muslim Education and the Scholar's Social Status*, Der Islām, Verlag and Shalaby, op. cit.
12. Tritton, op. cit., p 15.
13. Shalaby, op. cit., pp 127-130.
14. Bernier, Francois (1891 CE), *Travels in the Mughal Empire* quoted in Keay, F.E., *A History of Education in India and Pakistan*, Oxford University Press, 1959 CE, pp 127-130.

Science Education and Religious Belief: some philosophical perceptions and practical strategies

Dr Nasim Butt

The scientific enterprise is erected upon a certain philosophical and metaphysical base which is seldom questioned by practising scientists. If, therefore, one removes oneself from the universal domain of the practising scientist and enters the parochial den of the philosopher of science, one is subjected to a deluge of questions about the nature and validity of scientific knowledge, and how this knowledge is achieved: what are the methods of science? How does science differ from other disciplines? What are facts, laws and theories? What is 'truth' in science? How does science progress? Answers posited to such questions have challenged the belief that scientific knowledge is *certain* knowledge about how nature works, revealed by careful, *completely objective* observation and measurement. Instead, a dynamic view of science emerges, in which man's creative imagination plays an important part and in which complete objectivity, although patiently striven for, can never be achieved. Although a considerable consensus among scientists exists about the knowledge which results from their activities, scientific knowledge is nevertheless tentative and uncertain and influenced by numerous social and cultural factors.

It is crucial to appreciate that scientific knowledge is not an objective, literal description of reality (no such description being possible), it is an uncertain and tentative way of *imagining* or *representing certain aspects* of reality. This view immediately suggests explanations for failures in Western science, the modern science practised almost universally, including those Muslim states ruled by westernised elites only too happy to emulate the West in the name of progress and development. Take, for example, the thalidomide case, the unwanted side-effects of science (such as pollution) and the progressive destruction of the stratospheric ozone layer through the excessive use of aerosols and refrigerator fluids produced as a result of the capitalist entrepreneurial tendency. Western science is a very narrow epistemological path: we must, therefore, be prepared for the unexpected when such partial knowledge possessing elements of uncertainty is technologically applied.

It is my belief that science cannot be taught without its value-laden philosophy. Science is not value-free, objective and neutral. In fact, in a post-Kuhnian world[1] it is untenable to talk about such an intellectually transcendental type of science. Every factual statement that science produces has a number of underlying assumptions which are usually unquestioned. Consider the fact, for instance, that 'pure water boils at 100°C at 101.3223 kN/M^2'. Could any honest and diligent person 'find' that fact, where 'find' means determine in some way other than looking it up in a book of data? The answer must be 'no', because before anyone could make such a statement after observing water boiling, he or she would have to have concepts of 'boiling', 'temperature' and 'pressure', know how to use a thermometer and have access to both a barometer and a supply of pure water. The conclusions to be drawn from this are (1) that facts are not 'things' but statements which are made after observation, (2) that observation in science may require the experienced use of tools, and (3) that statements of fact incorporate concepts which must be understood before the statements can be made. Clearly, such facts are not simply 'found' in nature.

It is a matter of great regret that existing science education locates in the students' minds an impression that this narrow epistemological path is the 'only' approach. It is my view that students should gain some understanding of the historical development and contemporary cultural significance of scientific principles and theories. They should also appreciate that past scientific explanations were valid in their own time and that early technologies are still valid in some cultural contexts. Unfortunately, however, much of school science as currently presented does not encourage the development of these aims.

I view with cautious optimism, therefore, statutory developments in the science curriculum. In the Programme of Study for Key Stage 4 (years 10 and 11 in accordance with the National Curriculum age grouping), under the heading History of Scientific Ideas[2], the statutory document states:

> Pupils should be given opportunities to develop their knowledge and understanding of the ways in which scientific ideas change through time and how the nature of these ideas and the use to which they are put are affected by the social, moral, spiritualand cultural contexts in which they are developed; in doing so they should begin to recognise that, while science is an important way of thinking about experience, it is not the only way. (1A)

These ideas have now been incorporated in Attainment Target 1 of the science curriculum, namely 'Experimental amd Investigative Science' (post-Dearing review developments. These are encouraging words from the Department for Education and Employment (DFEE), but how and in what way they will be implemented in schools remains to be seen. Suffice it to say here that Muslim science teachers and educationists have the opportunity to play an important and constructive role in the implementation of this key passage. Subsequent paragraphs will show why.

Current science texts retain some Greek names, notably that of Archimedes, but the emphasis is on 17th, 18th and 19th century science. The names in a secondary school physics book might include the following: Galileo (1564 – 1642 CE), Boyle (1627 – 1691 CE), Hooke (1635 – 1703 CE), Newton (1642 – 1727 CE), Coulomb (1736 – 1806 CE), Watt (1736 – 1819 CE), Volta (1745 – 1827 CE), Young (1773 – 1829 CE), Ohm (1789 – 1854 CE), Faraday (1791 – 1867 CE), Ampere (1800 – 1864 CE), Joule (1818 – 1889 CE), Kelvin (1824 – 1907 CE) and Maxwell (1831 – 1879 CE). Very little is ever made of the cultural contexts in which they worked and, more significantly, no reference at all is made to the seminal work in science and technology performed by Muslim scientists such as Ibn Sinā (d. 1036 CE), Ibn al-Haithām (d. 1040 CE), Al-Birūnī (d. 1051 CE), Ibn Rushd (d. 1198 CE) and Ibn Nafīs (d. 1288 CE).

School chemistry and biology are equally culpable. Chemistry, for example, dismisses the contribution of early chemists by labelling them 'alchemists'. Yet it is clearly nonsense to believe that all early scientists were only trying to make gold, or that they did not lay the sound foundations upon which Dalton (1766 – 1844 CE) and others could base the atomic theory. The work of the Muslim chemist Jabir Ibn Hayyān (d. c. 815 CE) is particularly relevant in this regard. Also, quite significantly, the fact that much of Newton's work could be termed 'alchemy' is conveniently ignored.

The danger inherent in the present situation, then, is that students can emerge from schools with negative images of the science of non-Western societies. More significant for us, however, is that Muslim students will emerge from schools with either a negative perception of Islāmic science or, perhaps equally disastrous, no perception of Islāmic science at all. It is crucial, therefore, for some history of science to be included in school science courses and, concomitantly, for European science to be placed in a world perspective instead of the present Eurocentric impression of a global enterprise universally applicable. In addition, posters displayed in the classroom or laboratory could help to create the necessary awareness which could also be reinforced with appropriate passages and illustrations from textbooks and, for Muslim scientists, the *Qur'ān*.

Students should also, I believe, explore topics or themes which exemplify the limitations of scientific knowledge. The notion of science as an omnipotent enterprise able to solve all man's problems is now a decadent idea. With the growth of the environmental lobby in the West, people are much more sceptical about the ability of science to improve the quality of their lives. The implications of producing transgenic organisms, the social and environmental catastrophe that modern technologies can bring about and the much-debated research on human embryos are all examples of topics which produce interactions between moral and scientific perceptions. In Islām, however, the students should understand that the religious perspective is much clearer. Indeed, in order to provide guidance to their scientists, early Islāmic philosophers attempted to classify sciences as either 'praiseworthy' or 'blameworthy'.

Students must be made aware of the fact that different civilizations have different world-views; that science and technology is a product of this (the Western) world-view and would consequently be underpinned by different assumptions in different civilisational contexts. This has been to some extent admitted by the Secondary Science Curriculum Review (SSCR) working under the aegis of the Association for Science Education (ASE) and the School Curriculum Development Committee (SCDC)[3]:

> Science is, after all, an activity of human beings, acting and interacting. In fact it is a social activity. Scientific endeavour, including the development of technology, is determined by the cultural, religious, environmental, political and economic factors, and it is an activity in which the entire human race has been and is involved.

The Islāmic perspective, of which the students should be aware, is that the epistemological unilateralism of Western science is just one aspect within the overall conceptual framework of knowledge. One of the best articulators of Islāmic epistemology was Imām Abū Ḥamid Muḥammad Al-Ghazālī (1058 – 1111 CE), who was a professor at the Nizamīya Academy in Baghdād. Al-Ghazālī analysed knowledge in his *Book of Knowledge* on the basis of three criteria:

1. **The source**
   (a) Revealed knowledge, acquired from the Prophets and not arrived at either by reason, like arithmetic, or by experimentation, like medicine, or by hearing, like languages.
   (b) Non-revealed knowledge, the primary sources of which are reason, observation, experimentation and acculturation.
2. **The level of obligatoriness**
   (a) Individually requisite knowledge *(Farḍ 'ain)*, that is, knowledge which is essential for an individual to survive, e.g. social ethics, morality, civil law.
   (b) Socially requisite knowledge *(Farḍ kifāyah)*, or what is essential for the survival of the whole community, e.g. agriculture, medicine, architecture, engineering.
3. **The social function**
   (a) Praiseworthy sciences, that is, those which are useful and indispensable sciences the knowledge of which activities of this life depend.
   (b) Blameworthy sciences, which would include astrology, magic, certain types of war sciences, aversion therapy, the scientific study of torture, etc.

It is, I believe, of crucial importance for students to understand that Western science is based on part 1(b) of this epistemological taxonomy. Reason became the transcendental value of the age of European enlightenment in the eighteenth century. Observation and experiment as the prime methodological tools, underpinned by reason as the prime conceptual tool, were to launch science on the path of irreversible progress and technological achievement. Francis Bacon's dictum that 'nature reveals its secrets under torture' is particular apposite in this connection.

Taking Al-Ghazālī's classification as a whole, it becomes clear why, in Islām, science and religious education are complementary. Islāmic epistemology is uncompromisingly and unreservedly holistic. The methodologies and conceptual tools of science cannot operate on their own, they need the framework of absolute truth – Divine Revelation – and they function within the ethical and moral injunctions and principles enunciated therein. This is the sort of science which is holistic, not reductionist; a science not envisaged as the universal panacea for humanity, having come the closest to truth that we can get, but as a conceptual tool very useful for solving some of humanity's problems, revelation being the transcendental truth to which the enterprise of Science is ultimately accountable. In short, this is the sort of science that is not in conflict with religion.

The rediscovery of the nature and style of Islāmic science in our time is one of the most exciting and intellectually requisite challenges facing Muslim societies. To this end, it is necessary to examine modern science and science policy within a framework of concepts that shape the goals of Muslim society. This exercise was attempted at a seminar on 'knowledge and values' held under the auspices of the International Federation of Institutes of Advanced Study (IFIAS) in Stockholm in September 1981.[4] The Seminar isolated ten Islāmic concepts which embrace and describe the nature of scientific enquiry: *tawhīd* (unity), *khilāfah* (man's trusteeship), *'ibādah* (worship), *'ilm* (knowledge), *ḥalāl* (legal), *ḥarām* (illegal), *'adl* (justice), *ẓulm* (tyranny), *istislah* (public interest) and *dhiya* (waste). In the words of Ziauddin Sardar:[5]

> The positive values act as guiding principles for scientific activity and science policy in Muslim cultures, while the negative values of *ḥarām*, *ẓulm* and *dhiya* act as indicators which point out that the legitimate boundaries of Islāmic science have been overstepped. The three central concepts of *tawhīd*, *khilāfah* and *'ibādah* shape the paradigm of Islāmic science. Within this paradigm, Islāmic science operates through the agency of *'ilm* to promote *'adl* and *istislah* and undermine *ẓulm* and *dhiya*.

Admittedly, this theoretical model of science is skeletal and needs to be fleshed-out and extensively elaborated before being operationalised as a science policy for Muslim countries. It should be noted that the concepts are not inflexible. Others could be added: for example, *taqwā* (God-consciousness), *Ākhirah* (the Hereafter) and *ijmā'* (consensus of the community) are obviously very important. This point, however, is marginal. The central objective should be to develop an Islāmic philosophy of science based on concepts such as these.

Within such an ethical and moral framework, faith and theory would not be compartmentalised. Students would be aware of the criteria of theory assessment and, therefore, may be in a position to evaluate the relative merits of competing theories. Prior to embarking on this intellectual endeavour, students should be aware that all that is destructive physically, materially and spiritually, is *ḥarām*, while all that promotes these human parameters is *ḥalāl*. Scientific activity should promote social justice and pay due regard to *istislah* (public interest), a chief supplementary source of Islāmic law. Conversely, scientific activity should not promote alienation and dehumanisation, concentration of wealth in fewer and fewer hands and environmental destruction. There is thus no need to avoid theories deemed to be anti-religious as their evaluation should prove to be intellectually stimulating and a productive exercise on the basis of the societal parameters outlined above.

This brings me to the religiously degrading and intellectually distorted attempt to legitimise modern science by equating it with the *Qur'ān*. This is done by pointing out that the *Qur'ān* places great emphasis on the pursuit of knowledge and use of reason, and that it mentions several scientific facts and theories, all of which are supported by recent discoveries and advances. The standard reference work which propagates this type of approach to science and Islām is *The Bible, the Qur'ān and Science* by Maurice Bucaille, a French surgeon.[6] This type of pseudo-intellectual analysis amounts to the following: if the statements and theories mentioned in the *Qur'ān*, which was revealed 1400 years ago, are supported by modern science, the Divine nature of the *Qur'ān* is confirmed; and if modern scientific theories find a reflection in the *Qur'ān*, then modern science must have the same universal validity as the *Qur'ān*.

Both propositions are palpably preposterous. By equating the *Qur'ān* with science, the latter is elevated to the realm of the Divine and makes revelation subject to the verification of Western science. If this proposition is taken to its ludicrous conclusion, the *Qur'ān* would be proved false if a particular scientific fact does not tally with it or if a particular fact mentioned in the *Qur'ān* is refuted by modern science. Such an approach, therefore, is to be strongly condemned. It raises science to the level of sacred knowledge, effectively undermining any criticism of it.

Apart from this type of pestiferous philosophy of science, we must realise that there are many books for students based on theories such as that of evolution. Our long-term aim, of course, should be to develop educational criteria and curriculum materials designed and suitable for Muslim students of all ages and aptitudes. In the meantime, however, I am of the opinion that the theory of evolution, as enunciated by Charles Darwin (1809 – 1882 CE)and others, should be taught precisely because it has exercised such a profound influence upon Western thought. Our students should have a clear view of the intellectual antecedents of the present Western society and culture. The Islāmic perspective, of course, should also be given, concisely and eloquently, at the same time that the dehumanising ways in which the evolutionary theory was used in the early part of the present century are pointed out.

Apart from such dehumanising abuse, further difficulties can arise with Darwin's theory of evolution when it introduces the ideas of 'natural selection' and 'survival of the fittest'. These ideas, applied to human evolution, portray a sequence leading from man as an ape-like creature through to stone-age man, the hunter gatherer and finally to modern man. The process may be seen as one of progress and, all too easily, modern man may be identified with the economically successful white man surrounded by his technological 'goodies', while hunter-gatherer or stone-age man may be identified with those in nomadic tribal societies often described as 'primitive'. Using this model, a hierarchy of races can be inferred. It is important to stress that in actuality we are very ignorant about the origins of different racial groups, and to direct the students' attention to the following verse of the *Qur'ān*:

> *O mankind,*
> *We have created you male and female,*
> *and have formed you into nations and tribes*
> *in order that you may know one another.*
> *The most honoured of you in the sight of Allāh*
> *is he who is most righteous.*
> *Indeed, Allāh is Knower, Aware.*[7]

In any case, whatever its reality for modern man, race is not a fact of Islāmic cognition. Indeed, the very idea of Islām is the antithesis of the race principle. The Islāmic conception of man is that he is essentially a moral being and only incidentally a construct of biology. The fundamental precept here is that, according to Islāmic cognition, the ultimate determinant of man's humanity is his morality, not his biology. That is to say, the ultimate worth of a person is determined by his or her righteousness (or *taqwā*). Human biological differences must be construed as the signs of *Allāh's* glory and bounty that add lustre and colour to mankind's cultural and ethnic diversity. Or, in the incomparable words of the *Qur'ān*:

> *Among His (Allāh's) signs*
> *are the creation of the Heaven and Earth,*
> *and the variety of your tongues and hues.*
> *Surely, in that are signs for those who know.*[8]

These concepts would not be imparted in an epistemologically parochial and reductionist education system. Hence the crucial need for Muslim teachers, scientists, scholars and educationists to understand the pedagogical underpinnings of the British education system, and to collectively produce materials which impart such a holistic awareness while at the same time fulfilling the requirements of the National Curriculum. As I mentioned earlier, it is my belief that an opportunity has now been provided which we should, as a community, take advantage of.

Faith cannot in any way be left at the door of the classroom. For a Muslim, Islām is a living reality within the framework of which all other systems and processes operate and find their meaning. It is not an imposition if the teacher's faith is manifested in classroom dialogue and curricular discussion. It is hypocrisy, however, as the fundamentally secular West has shown us, to compartmentalise faith, and practise a politically handicapped and claustrophobic religion reduced to ritual and theological disputations. In Islām, every act is carried out for the pleasure of *Allāh*; this is the essence of *Imān* (faith). The practice of science and the art of teaching are no exception to this universal ethical precept.

> *We (Allāh) will show them the signs in all regions of the Earth*
> *and in themselves,*
> *until they come to see that this is the truth.*[9]

1. See T.S. Kuhn, *The Structure of Scientific Revolutions*, The University of Chicago Press, 1962.
2. *Science for Ages 5 to 16 (1991)*, Proposals of the Secretary of State for Education and Science and the Secretary of State for Wales, DES May 1991, p44. See also the recent slimmed-down version of the science curriculum, post-Dearing review, incorporating these ideas in the preamble to key stages 3 and 4.
3. *Science Education for a Multicultural Society*, Leicestershire Education Authority, 1986.
4. The discussion of the Stockholm seminar is reported in *The Touch of Midas: Science, Values and Environment in* Islām *and the West,* edited by Ziauddin Sardar, Manchester University Press, 1984.
5. Z. Sardar, Islām*ic Futures: the Shape of Ideas to Come,* Mansell Publishing Limited, 1985, pp 175-176.
6. Maurice Bucaille, *The Bible, the Qur'ān and Science*, Seghers, Paris, 1980.
7. *Al-Qur'ān*, chapter 49, verse 13.
8. *Ibid.*, chapter 30, verse 22.
9. *Ibid.*, chapter 41, verse 53.

Islāmising University Education: problems and prospects

PROF SYED SAJJAD HUSAIN

The view that the Western system of education and the values it imparts are different from, and even antithetical to, the Muslim concept of the good life has been with us ever since the beginning of the East's colonial history. When the Western colonial powers introduced their languages and their system of education in the areas they controlled, they let the old traditional systems continue in parallel with the new schools and colleges, so that to this day in all Muslim countries we have a kind of diarchy or dualism in education. The traditional schools (or *madrasahs*, as they are called) serve as theological seminaries and follow syllabuses that have remained unreformed for centuries. They teach no new subjects, eschew science and modern philosophy and are centred on Islāmic religious texts, the *Qur'ān* and the *Ahādīth*, turning out graduates who find it difficult to adapt to modern institutions. Whilst their role in the preservation of Islāmic learning is understood and appreciated, the process of modernisation that Muslim societies have been forced to adopt relies on the products of modern colleges and universities, some of whom seem almost totally alienated from Islāmic moorings. The phenomenon of parallel systems is to be found in Egypt, the Indian subcontinent, Iran, Malaysia, Indonesia and the (former Soviet) Central Asian Republics. Now that modern education has been introduced to Saudi Arabia as well, the same dualism has been replicated on Arab soil.

It is against this background that the question of Islāmising university education has to be considered and understood.

Those who insist on Islāmisation do not want modern universities to be scrapped and replaced by *madrasahs*. Nor do they advocate a boycott of Western education like the Muslim *'Ulamā* in India in the nineteenth century who initially condemned Western learning as Satanical and persuaded many Muslims to give it a wide berth in the interest of their faith. It took men like Sir Syed Aḥmad and Nawab 'Abdul Latīf years to convince their co-religionists of the folly of this policy which had begun to deprive the Muslims of all opportunities of getting on in life. Each step they took had to be carefully measured, for the feeling that Western education cuts a young man or woman off from their society was strong. At Aligarh, in north India, Sir Syed created what he thought to be an Islāmic version of Oxford colleges, where students could receive Western education in a setting which, outwardly at least, had an Islāmic look.

Sir Syed planned a reconciliation between Western and Islāmic learning by assuming that they could work in tandem, that a Muslim could be steeped in Islāmic culture and, at the same time, study Western science, philosophy and English. He himself, in his writings, sought to interpret Islām in terms which were intended to demonstrate that there was no basic opposition between modern science and the teachings of the *Qur'ān*. His commentary on Ghazālī's philosophy aims to disclose flaws in the latter's system which he considered indefensible.

Sir Syed's advocacy of Western education and, in particular, his belief that the *Qur'ān* was not at variance with science, earned him much opprobrium from some of his contemporaries. Some went so far as to question his faith in Islām, even whilst acknowledging his services as an educationist and political thinker. Those who did not dismiss him as an enemy of Islām, but were not prepared to accept all his ideas, thought he was apologetic in his approach. It was said that he proceeded from the premise that Muslim suspicion about the drift of modern science was groundless.

The writings of Syed Ameer 'Ali (particularly *The Spirit of* Islām and *The History of the Saracens*) provoked a similar reaction in some quarters. He too was said to be apologetic in his attitude.

However, by and large it was the school of thought represented by Sir Syed and his younger contemporary Ameer 'Ali that triumphed over the old *madrasahs*. In spite of what the *'Ulamā* at Deoband in India and other religious seminaries preached, ever larger numbers of Muslims flocked to modern schools and colleges to gain a knowledge of English and modern science. The seminaries have not died out but, whilst they have been responsible for what I have called a diarchy in Muslim education, their impact on administration and culture has ceased to be a matter of any consequence. Al-Azhar in Egypt, which enjoys the reputation of being the greatest centre of Islāmic learning, is increasingly being overshadowed, if our information is correct, by modern universities and colleges, and has been obliged to introduce a modern syllabus to run alongside the traditional one.

To understand the difference between the *madrasahs* and modern universities it is necessary to realise that it is not merely a dissimilarity in the matter of syllabuses. The *madrasahs* represent a world view in which the changes in our conception of the material universe, changes that we owe to science, are not reflected. The astronomy they teach is pre-Galilean; their geology has not gone beyond the findings of medieval scholars; they reject modern historical methodology where it seems to threaten legends embedded in the consciousness of our ancestors; their logic invokes Aristotle as the last word in analysis; their hermeneutics would not at all admit the validity of modern methods of textual scrutiny and interpretation; their concept of history as a discipline would rather ignore the labours of archaeologists and anthropologists than acknowledge that what is recorded in books written centuries ago could contain errors.

The distinguishing feature of traditional Muslim education, the critics say, is that it offers given judgements and would not like them to be questioned. The pupil's duty according to the old system is to absorb rather than question; to assimilate rather than analyse; to memorise rather than try to understand rationally. The *madrasah* system is, however, a comprehensive fabric with its base in elementary education and its apex in courses corresponding to modern post-graduate education. It also projects a consistent world view rather than the kind of empirical deductions which form the staple of modern education. It is, to give it its due, a full-fledged alternative to modern education.

I have devoted all this space to a discussion of the main features of traditional Muslim education in order to bring to light an ambiguity or paradox which lies at the heart of the demand for Islāmisation being voiced in certain Muslim circles today. They do not urge a return to traditional education as our *'Ulamā* did in the 19th and early 20th centuries. If not directly and openly, they acknowledge implicitly the utility of modern Western education; they would not reject science and technology as such but insist that there is an alternative, an Islāmic alternative, which needs to be discovered and substituted for them. Nor do they reject modern philosophy as such; they assert that within the framework of thought organised on modern lines, Islāmic concepts of political rights, economic justice, historical analysis, anthropological research, sociological theory and so on can – or must – be found so as to rescue Muslim youth from the meretricious lure of Western life which is totally at variance with the ideals laid down in the *Qur'ān* and the teachings of the Prophet.

The late Dr Ismā'īl Rāji Al-Fārūqī, one of the pioneers who held strong views on the subject, rejects even the term 'Social Sciences' in the statement he wrote on Islāmisation. Those who participated in the Kuala Lumpur Conference on Islāmisation, which was one of a series, also reiterated the opinion that the whole scheme of education followed in modern universities needed to be recast and remoulded on Islāmic lines because, they protested, no branch of Western knowledge was value-free. Not even the sciences, they said. Not even architecture. Everything that has come out of the Western crucible bears the stamp of a culture which is imbued with either Christian, pagan or atheistic ideology.

This criticism is not at all different from the objections that led Muslim *'Ulamā* in India in the 19th century to advocate the boycott of Western schools. But whereas the 19th century *'Ulamā* called upon the community to stick to the *madrasah* system, the modern critics shy away from prescribing the same remedy. Nor, as far as I have been able to determine, do they have a comprehensive scheme like the *madrasah* system to suggest as an alternative.

It will perhaps be readily agreed that no system of education can be understood in a vacuum without reference to the social milieu in which it functions. That the Western system should reflect the values of Western society is not to be wondered at, but there is one respect where all systems converge. They make a distinction between primary and higher education. Children need to be subjected to a process which is little different from plain indoctrination. They have to be initiated into the values that a society cherishes by means which deny them any choice between what to accept and what to reject. A child has to learn to count, it has to acquire the alphabet, it needs to learn how to dress, eat in the accepted way, how to sit and so on. Training of this kind is basic, and if it were left to the children to decide whether assimilating the traditional alphabet is the right way of acquiring a language or whether they should invent a new alphabet, there would be no education at all. But higher education meant for young adults presupposes a much greater degree of choice. The purpose here is to enable the young to understand rationally the foundations on which their society rests; blind acceptance is at this stage much less important than freedom of enquiry. This vital distinction between the two stages needs to be kept constantly in view.

One of the chief attractions of Western education at higher stages is that whereas in the *madrasah* system from beginning to end the main emphasis is on faith and submission to given judgements, the learner in the Western system is called upon to use his reason to probe what he is offered; he is told that doubt is the first condition of knowledge.

Unless we desire to install the *madrasah* system in a new setting, we must try and understand what the implications of Islāmisation will be.

There are scholars like the late Dr Ismā'īl Rāji Al-Fārūqī who, without admitting that the *madrasah* alternative has been found unsuitable in the context of the modern world, insist on rejecting the entire scheme of Western education to the extent of not even using the term 'social sciences'. Speakers at the Kuala Lumpur conference, as I have said, inveighed against almost every branch of Western knowledge in analogous terms.

While I agree that something needs to be done to arrest the erosion of Islāmic values among university students, I feel somewhat confused when I consider the recommendations of these scholars. They appear to me to mistake methods of research for its findings in both the humanities and the sciences. They urge the necessity of indoctrination at higher stages in the same manner in which for over seventy years the communists in Russia and elsewhere enforced the teaching of Marxist thought in all disciplines. Every student in the USSR admitted to a university, whether from outside or from within the country, had to submit to a process of immersion in Marxism in order that he might acquire the ability to judge every problem from a definite Marxist angle. The result, as the erstwhile communists themselves agree, has been stagnation, distortion and falsification, all of which combined to bring about the disaster which the communist world now faces.

It is certainly not my purpose to equate Islām with Marxism. But I am afraid that those who think that, its basic beliefs apart, there is an immutable Islāmic perspective in every area, misinterpret Islām'*s* approach to knowledge, and are advocating something totally different from the broad-minded outlook that characterised our forebears in the early history of our faith. The Arabs who were the first to come in contact with the Greek world intellectually did not reject Plato and Aristotle right away; they assimilated Greek science and philosophy but constructed systems of thought that reflected their own basic religious beliefs. There was no attempt to divide knowledge into compartments, Islāmic and un-Islāmic, and shun whole areas of research for fear that such investigations might lead to results which might at first prove difficult to reconcile with faith.

The weaknesses in the argument in favour of wholesale Islāmisation at higher levels of education appear to me to fall into several categories.

First, I do not agree that knowledge can be classified as Islāmic or non-Islāmic or, for that matter, into Christian and non-Christian, or pagan and non-pagan. Knowledge implies understanding the universe we inhabit, and no one but a fool will ever claim that man can or has been able to comprehend the whole of the mystery that is the universe. While men of faith attribute real knowledge to God alone, others resort to agnosticism to account for the same ignorance as to the nature of reality. The frontiers of human understanding have advanced from age to age, but each advance in knowledge reveals further riddles which continue to baffle us. To say, therefore, that all Western learning is value-charged is to confuse knowledge with the uses to which Western man has put his acquirements to consolidate and perpetuate his power, to buttress his imperialist conquests, to provide justification for his racial bias, to belittle the achievements of others even where Western scholars in their sober moments acknowledge their debt to Oriental sources. But notwithstanding this tendency to distortion and concealment, historians with any degree of intellectual honesty admit that civilisation is a many-layered structure consisting of deposits, each resting on or having its foundation in what has gone before. If the Arabs in the Middle Ages did not reject Greek science and philosophy on the grounds that they came from pagan sources, neither did Western man refuse to accept the findings of Arab science and philosophy. But, unfortunately for us, a kind of intellectual torpor descended on the Muslim world sometime during the 16th and 17th centuries, and creative activity amongst Muslims practically ceased. This was a reaction to political defeat, as political defeat was accelerated by the cessation of creativity. Newton, Huygens, Planck and Einstein have no counterparts in the Islāmic world. We do not have an Edison, a Pasteur or a Lister; nor do we have a Rutherford or a Ford. Are we to cover up our lack of progress in science and industry by pleading that we must shun modern electricity, telegraphy, radio and the innumerable inventions which we now use?

The participants in the Kuala Lumpur conference, as well as the late Dr Rāji, Dr Hossein Nasr and other proponents of Islāmisation seem to me to content themselves with abstract criticism rather than descend to the concrete and declare in precise terms where the line between Islāmic and non-Islāmic knowledge must be drawn.

One of the participants in the said conference, Hussein M. Ateshin, strongly criticised Western architectural concepts taught to Cairo University students. Western architecture naturally reflects Western concepts of beauty, but is it possible to deny that architectural creations are dictated as much by the architect's aesthetic ideas as by the state of technology at any given stage? The Alhambra, the Taj, the Badshahi Mosque in Delhi and the Qutb Minar in the same city are very different from the earliest monuments erected in Madīnah, as are the King Faisal Mosque in Islāmabad, the Regent's Park Mosque in London and the Washington Islāmic Center. Is the use of electricity in mosques and the installation of modern plumbing to be regarded as sacrilege? The Gothic churches in Europe differ in design and look from mosques in Iran, Turkey, Central Asia, India and the North African countries but they are alike in using the principle of the arch, which was invented by pagans. To give one more example: multi-storied buildings in the modern world have been made possible by advances in technology of which neither the West nor the East had any knowledge even in the 19th century. Can we truthfully say that they have been religiously inspired? They can be, and have been, criticised on various grounds, but I believe that to condemn high-rise architecture as un-Islāmic would be to betray the same confusion of ends and means that I have referred to earlier.

Take another technological invention which has revolutionised civilisation: printing. Printing has advanced far from the days of its originators in China, or the time of Gutenburg and Caxton. In Europe it helped in the diffusion of Biblical knowledge, but this did not prevent the Muslims from using it with the plea that those who developed printing in Europe had a religious motive in mind.

What I am driving at is that the sweeping condemnation of modern technology and science which has become the staple of recent protests against Western colonialism actually clouds the real issue and is based on wrong and unprovable premises. I wonder how one could maintain that men like Kepler, Tycho Brahe and Galileo, who risked their necks by challenging the astronomical theories cherished by the Catholic Church, were deliberately trying to promote any cultural imperialism. Newton was a believing Christian but his theories cannot be shown to have been inspired by any religious impulse.

Knowledge is neutral but there is no area of knowledge that cannot be used for wrong and immoral purposes. The executioner's sword which can be used to impose the death penalty on criminals can also be a tool in the hands of murderers.

The social sciences (or 'Ummatic sciences' as Dr Rāji calls them) appear to be different in this respect. However, the difference is superficial. Consider, for example, historiography, which is a matter of organising and interpreting facts. There is a Christian interpretation, as there is a Marxist interpretation, and there are interpretations which differ from both. Arnold Toynbee thought history represented a series of challenges and responses. We are aware that Ibn Khaldūn in the 14th century saw history differently. But the basic question which cannot be ignored is that historiography should not involve deliberate distortion and must be based on proven and provable facts. Bias of one sort or another is perhaps impossible to eliminate, for historiography is not an exact science. But the methods of analysis, the sifting of evidence which over the centuries has led to the differentiation of legend from fact, are tools in the hands of scholars which can be, and have been, used differently by different historians. The accusation that this methodology is value-charged is untenable because it has on numerous occasions been employed by non-Muslim writers in their disputes with one another. No Christian writer today would defend without qualification Bede who wrote a history of the English church in the 8th century, or the Chronicles of Froissart, or the accounts of the Crusades written by Joinville and Villehardouin. Herodotus and Livy are judged differently from Thucydides and Tacitus. Mommsen, Ranke, Gibbon, Macaulay, Croce, Braudel – no one escapes continuous scrutiny, and they are apt to be evaluated differently as new research discloses new data, though from the Muslim point of view they might all appear to project a world view which is anti-Muslim.

What I mean is that while a Muslim must beware of being won over by a judgement which gives a slant to facts, he has to make a distinction between methods of research and their interpretation.

In political science and economics, the difference between Muslim perspectives and Christian/non-Muslim views is bound to be sharper. But again the distinction between methods of analysis and the interpretations must not be lost sight of.

The solution to the dilemma the Muslims face in higher education in modern universities is not the imposition of a rigid pattern of knowledge in the name of Islāmisation, a pattern that will admit of no deviations. For one thing, the moment we sit down to work out a scheme in detail we will be confronted by the insuperable difficulty of agreeing among ourselves as to what the Islāmic view is. The *Ummah* today numbers over a billion, spread over several continents and representing a diversity of races, languages and cultural traditions. The differences between *Shia* and *Sunni* are paralleled by differences between the various schools of thought in both groups. If it is objected that all Muslims accept belief in God and faith in the Prophethood of Muḥammad ﷺ, we have to reckon with the fact that the unfortunate but historically inevitable fragmentation of the *Ummah* into national units has been characterised by internecine strife between one Muslim group and another, and a common Islāmic perspective in these areas will be impossible to achieve.

Secondly, unless we advocate a reversion to the old *madrasah* system, where some kind of unity of outlook can be perceived, and unless we think that a multiplication of the sort of university that the Saudi government has created in Madīnah for the study of the *Qur'ān* and the *Sunnah* (which really is a *madrasah* with a different name) can help us Islāmise knowledge, we cannot avoid modernisation; this implies the acceptance of the world of knowledge that has come to be thought of as Western not, however, uncritically. The bitter and unpalatable truth that it is by mastering modern science and technology and philosophy that the Muslims can survive has, frankly, to be recognised and faced. The Muslim world's experience in the Gulf War of 1991 underlined the causes of our weaknesses. To put a false gloss on these weaknesses by preaching the theory that there exists an Islāmic alternative to every branch of knowledge is not only to mislead the Muslim public but also to encourage communal suicide.

The main cause of the erosion of Islāmic values among the young at universities lies in our failure, even in such Muslim countries as Pakistan and Bangladesh, to enforce a system of primary and secondary education that is designed to impregnate children at an impressionable age with basic Islāmic principles. In Bangladesh, thanks to the erroneous educational policies adopted by successive administrations from the fifties onwards, a generation has grown up to whom Islām is unknown except as a legend. They are less conscious of their spiritual and cultural heritage as Muslims than even some Muslim children in Britain who have been forced by the pervasive hostility towards their identity in the society they live in to rediscover the validity of their own culture. That a thorough grounding in the basics at primary education level pays excellent dividends is amply demonstrated by the fact that few Saudi scholars exposed to higher education in American and British universities, whether in the humanities or the sciences, return wholly brainwashed. I spent ten years teaching in Makkah and in the course of that decade I remember encountering only one young man who had accepted Western values lock, stock and barrel. On the other hand, at home in Bangladesh where I taught in the University of Dhaka for 21 years from 1948 to 1969, each new generation of students coming up with an increasingly changing background in primary and secondary education seemed further away from Islām than its predecessor. They lacked elementary knowledge about Islām and even resented being reminded that the roots of their culture were to be found in their religion.

It is at this level that the problem has to be tackled. Where governmental help is unavailable, Muslim society must depend on private initiatives, as Muslim communities in Britain, France and the USA are doing. The scale of these initiatives will, of course, be determined by the nature of the challenge in each case. I am firmly persuaded that to neglect the base of the educational pyramid and run after false mirages at its top will mean stagnation, retardation and ever greater dependence on the West and its science and technology.

Parallel to efforts by government or non-government organisations at lower levels, a determined and well-planned effort is called for at higher levels to promote outstanding Muslim scholarship on a par with the competence of Western scholars, to produce books that will expose the inaccuracies to which the Muslims object. It is idle to fulminate against Western scholars without being able to demonstrate by positive action that

Muslims are capable of looking at the world differently. This has to be an intellectual exercise instead of being an exercise in polemics and rhetoric. The right answer to Orientalists like Goldziher, Muir, Montgomery Watt and Cantwell Smith, to name but a few, is not to thunder against them from various platforms but to accompany our vocal protests with books of the highest intellectual standard by Muslim scholars which, by virtue of their quality, will be read by all. Shoddy scholarship, however well-intentioned, will not do. I am afraid that little along these lines has so far been attempted.

Indictments of the concept of progress are often used to conceal our intellectual incompetence, our failure to produce competent works and make advances in knowledge. This is the malady that needs to be remedied. Those who inveigh against progress are unconsciously inspired by the fear that advances in knowledge might demolish their pet theories about Islām. There is a kind of indefensible conservatism at work which would not tolerate any challenge to ideas and theories which have come from mediaeval Muslim scholars. Not only men like Sir Syed Aḥmad and Syed Ameer 'Ali, whom I have mentioned before, but also even Iqbal did not escape suspicion about their loyalty to the basic tenets of Islām. We stand more or less where the Christian world in Europe stood at the end of the mediaeval period when any interpretation of dogma which deviated from the teaching of the Church Fathers was condemned as heretical. Interestingly, even St. Thomas Aquinas, the greatest Christian thinker of the Middle Ages, had to contend with some animosity at first, although today he is regarded in the Catholic Church as the very basis of authentic Christianity. Human knowledge is a constantly changing process in the humanities as well as the sciences; nothing the source of which is man can ever stand still. To imagine that a set of books written in the twentieth century will forever solve the problem of Islāmisation is to nurse an illusion. Every new generation of Muslims must be prepared to re-examine knowledge in the light of their understanding to keep pace with advances outside the community. Torpor and stagnation will confront us with the same dilemma in every age.

I propose to conclude this discussion with one of the most impressive examples that I have come across of childhood upbringing causing a complete reversal of a man's outlook late in life. Those who have read the works of Alexis Carrel, a Nobel Laureate, who returned to Christianity after a lifetime of disbelief and scepticism, realise with a shock how belief planted early can, at any age, enable a person to turn around. Carrel's *Man the Unknown* discusses human anatomy but in a perspective which is designed to bring to light mysteries which only religion recognises. His knowledge of the subject is impossible to fault but he arrives at a reconciliation between faith and science which astonishes by its reach. As I read him he seemed to remind me more than once of those Muslim thinkers in the past who excluded nothing from their purview, and succeeded in producing works whose intellectual competence no contemporary could question.

(Prof Syed Sajjad Husain passed away in 1995)

The Problems of Teaching Islāmic History

Dr Muhammad Abdul Jabbar Beg

Islāmic history began as an oral history among the disciples *(Ṣaḥābah)* of Prophet Muḥammad ﷺ. Whenever they met one another, it was their habit to ask questions about the latest happenings in the life of the Prophet and his instructions to members of the community *(Ummah)*, and to transmit the information orally from person to person. This process of transmission of news and views about the Prophet and his activities was a daily occurrence in the life of the Muslim community of Makkah before the *Hijrah*, and in Madīnan society after the emigration of Prophet Muḥammad ﷺ. This method of transmitting news, views and revelations received by the Prophet came to be known as the *ḥadīth* (pl. *aḥādīth*) or Traditions. Thus Islāmic history germinated in the oral transmission of the Prophet's ideas, activities and approbations during most of the first Islāmic century (seventh century CE). From oral Traditions, written versions were made by collectors of the Traditions. Thus, the idea of Islāmic history was born in the '*ḥadīth* paradigm' in early Islāmic society. By the term *ḥadīth* paradigm we imply the adoption of the methodology of *ḥadīth* by early Muslim historians. A *ḥadīth* has two basic parts, namely *isnād* (chain of narrators) and *matn* (lit. text, which referred to the saying, doing and approbation of the Prophet). Early Islāmic historians including al-Ṭabarī (d. 923 CE) have followed the methodology of the science of *ḥadīth* in collecting, sifting and accepting historical information. One basic element of a Tradition is *isnād* or chain of narrators, which traced back the report of the event to an eyewitness. Each transmitter of the information had to be a trustworthy person whose credibility depended on his reputation and character. The biographies of the transmitters of Traditions were known as *Asmā' al-rijāl* which preserved critical biographical accounts of each narrator of a saying of the Prophet and events in his life. The early Islāmic historians, following the example of the Traditionists *(muḥaddithūn)*, prepared complete dossiers about the persons who narrated historical information. Thus the early Muslim historians adopted the methodology of the *ḥadīth* collectors in laying down the foundation of early Islāmic historiography. 'Abd al-'Azīz al-Dūrī discussed the circumstances leading to the writing of history among the Arabs in his book, *Baḥth fī nash'at 'Ilm al-ta'rīkh 'ind al-'Arab.*[1]

The raw material of Islāmic history was transmitted orally by the disciples of the Prophet to their contemporaries and to the next generation during the first Islāmic century. During the second Islāmic century written compilations of historical information and records were available in the form of reports of the battles of the Prophet *(Maghāzī)* and the details of his blessed life in the form of *Sīrah* (biography). The *Ṣaḥābah* were the first-generation Muslims, who were eyewitness reporters and transmitters of historical information.

We would search in vain for the origins of Arabic/Islāmic historiography in the pre-Islāmic Arabic poetry called 'the register of the Arabs' *(al-Shi'ru Dīwān al-'Arab)*, or in the tribal genealogies *(Ansāb)* or in the ancient Yemenite folklore of the Himyarite Kings. These were minor factors in the formation of historical outlook of the Arabs before the advent of Islām. The birth of history in the Arabian society began with the public activities of Prophet Muḥammad ﷺ.The knowledge of the Prophet's biography was regarded as sacred knowledge because frequent reference was made to the statements of the Prophet on religious practices and legal precepts. An early Islāmic scholar, Abu'l-Husain ibn Fāris (d. c. 1000 CE), stated emphatically that, "every Muslim ought to have a very thorough knowledge of the biography of Muhammad ﷺ in all its details." Moreover, we can get an idea of the importance of history in Islāmic civilisation from the following statement by an Andalusian Muslim scholar, Abū Bakr Muḥammad al-Khamis (d. 1239

CE), who was reported to have said, "Next to the *Qur'ān* and the *Sunnah*, the subject deserving of utmost attention is history and biography." Imām al-Bukhārī (d. 870 CE), the most famous collector of Traditions, had a special knowledge of early Islāmic history. He used to sit near the pulpit of the Prophet's Mosque at Madīnah and write his great history *(Ta'rīkh al-Kabīr)*, a book of *Asmā' al-rijāl* about the lives of early Muslims, and record the collection of the *Jāmi' al-Ṣaḥīḥ* alternately during day and moonlit nights. He used to pray two *rak'ahs* of prayer after writing down a *ḥadīth* or a piece of historical information about the *Ṣaḥābah* sitting near the tomb of the Prophet. For Imām Bukhārī the writing of history and the *Jāmi' al-Ṣaḥīḥ* (authentic Traditions) were of equal merit. Thus the history of Prophet Muḥammad ﷺ and his disciples was invested with an aura of sanctity in the early Islāmic period. According to the information collected and recorded by the Muslim historian al-Sakhawī (d. 1497 CE), Islāmic history was treated by some Muslim scholars as an essential subject, and its preservation and transmission were the collective duty of the Muslim community *(Farḍ Kifāyah)*.[2]

The Arabic generic term for history is *ta'rīkh*, which literally means an era or a date. The introduction of the term *ta'rīkh* in Islāmic society coincided with the adoption of the Islāmic calendar after the *Hijrah* (lit. emigration) of Prophet Muḥammad ﷺ from Makkah to Madīnah. The Muslim leader responsible for the introduction of the Islāmic calendar or *ta'rīkh* was Khalīfah 'Umar ibn al-Khaṭṭāb (d. 644 CE), *raḍi Allāhu 'anhu*, in the seventeenth year (638 CE) after the *Hijrah*.[3] Sakhawī has reviewed the variety of historical writings in Islāmic civilisation in a treatise entitled *al-I'lān bi'l-tawbīkh li-man dhamma al-ta'rīkh* which literally means 'An open denunciation of the adverse critics of history'.[4] And the Arab historian Ibn Khaldūn (d. 1406 CE), among many other historians, has given us a clear definition of history as follows: "History refers to events that are peculiar to a particular age or race."[5] There are of course other definitions of history by Islāmic historians. For instance, the Turkish historian Tashkopruzadeh (d. 1561 CE) defined history as a branch of learning about various groups of people, their countries, laws and customs, handicrafts and professions and the genealogies of the people as well as their chronologies. He also described the scope of history as covering famous persons such as the prophets, saints, theologians, philosophers and physicians *(ḥukamā')*, kings and sultans[6] and such like.

Although Muslim historians had a clear perception of history, it was not often that they tried to define the subject. In other words, definitions of history are rather rare in Islāmic scholarship.

The teaching of Islāmic history in Muslim countries today faces many problems arising from two contrasting systems of education. The dichotomy in the education system has given rise to different approaches to the teaching methods of Islāmic history. The two approaches may be described as the traditional and the modern. The traditional approach is associated with the *Madrasah* education system, wherein Islāmic history is treated as a branch of theology *(Uṣūl al-Dīn)*. The books on history most commonly followed and recommended by the *'ulamā'* (Muslim theologians) are the *Sīrah Rasūl Allāh* (Biography of Muḥammad *Rasūl Allāh*) by Ibn Isḥāq (d. 767 CE) in the recension of Ibn Hishām (d. 834 CE) and the *Ta'rīkh al-Khulafā'* (History of the Caliphs) by Jalāl al-Dīn al-Suyūṭī (d. 1505 CE). Some *Madrasahs* also recommend Ahmad Amin's (d. 1954 CE) popular history books, *Fajr al-Islām* (The dawn of Islām), *Ḍuḥa'l-Islām* (Forenoon of Islām) and *Ẓuhr al-Islām* (Afternoon of Islām). It was probably with the *Madrasah* approach to Islāmic history in view that some modern scholars have made the devastating criticism that "the Muslim view of early Islāmic history is static and unproductive."[7] Such a general criticism of Islāmic history, in our view, is not appropriate.

Although some *Madrasah* teachers and a few university lecturers recommend Suyūṭī's *Ta'rīkh al-Khulafā'* as a reference work, it is hardly an ideal textbook, being full of incorrect chronology and misinterpretations of events. This history book gives a brief outline of the history of the Caliphs from Abū Bakr (d. 634 CE) to 'Alī (d. 660 CE), Umayyads (661 – 750 CE), 'Abbasids (750 – 1258 CE) and the shadow Caliphs of the 'Abbasid dynasty under the tutelage of the Mamluke sultans (1260 – 1516 CE) of Egypt up to the end of the 15th century CE. The book covered nine hundred years of the history of the Caliphs providing a bird's eye view of the Islāmic state till the last years of the author's life. This is a theologian's manual of Islāmic history which did not make his students and readers good historians. For instance, Suyūṭī's history shows the professional *'ulamā's* proclivity to narrate anecdotes and cite undigested information as quotations. He covered the history of the Fāṭimids (909 – 1171 CE) and Umayyad Spain (756 – 1031 CE) in three pages only. The author of this history book lacked critical judgement on historical developments, provided insufficient and often inaccurate chronology of events relating to Islāmic conquests which were fully documented by historians such as al-Balādhurī (d. 892 CE) in his *Kitāb Futūḥ al-Buldān*, and in the history of al-Ṭabarī. Among the traditional historians we also include Shams al-Dīn al-Dhahabī (d. 1348 CE), Ibn al-'Imād al-Ḥanbalī (d. 1678 CE) and others, but Ṭabarī's *Ta'rīkh al-Rusul wa'l-Mulūk* (History of the Prophets and Kings) and Ibn al-Athīr's (d. 1232 CE) *al-Kāmil fi'l-Ta'rīkh* (The Perfect book of History) have not been so popular with the traditional *'ulamā'*. Incidentally, the entire corpus of *Ta'rīkh al-Rusul wa'l-Mulūk* has recently been translated into English by a team of Orientalists and Muslim scholars as the History of al-Ṭabarī[8] (ed. by Yar-Shater, State University of New York Press) in thirty-eight volumes. The traditional approach to Islāmic history is as archaic as the *Madrasah* system of education in some countries. Ahmad Shalaby of Al-Azhar University in Cairo and his colleagues are recent protagonists of the traditional approach to Islāmic history. Shalaby largely adopted Suyūṭī's approach to the subject. On the other hand, there is a modern approach to Islāmic history which is closely associated with the school of Orientalists. In most of the universities of the Muslim world the modern approach to Islāmic history is now practised. Furthermore, the work of the Orientalists and that of Western historians of the Muslim countries has contributed to the introduction of Islāmic History as a subject in some European and American universities. The Orientalists' approach to Eastern knowledge in general and to that of Islāmic history in particular is based on oriental classics. The Orientalists rely on a philological approach to the old historical, literary or religious texts of the Orient. Although Orientalism is in decline, some of their books are used as reference material for Islāmic and Middle Eastern history in many parts of the Muslim world.

During the nineteenth and early part of the twentieth century, the Islāmic peoples were in political decline and many parts of the Islāmic world were colonised by European powers such as Great Britain and France. Colonialism provided an opportunity for Europeans to come into close contact with the Muslims of Asia and Africa. While the Christian missionaries were busy with efforts to conquer Muslim souls, and colonial entrepreneurs were busy robbing the Muslim nations of their natural and cultural resources, there arose a group of Western scholars who learnt the Oriental languages as a key to understanding the Orient. These European scholars who thrived under European colonialism and thereafter, were known as Orientalists. A brief digression on Orientalism may be in order now. In a recent publication on Orientalism, Edward Said defined the concept and function of the Orientalists: "Anyone who teaches, writes about or researches the Orient – and this applies whether the person is an anthropologist, sociologist, historian or philologist – each in its specific or its general aspects, is an Orientalist, and what he or she does is Orientalism."[9] From the point of view of this Arab critic, "Orientalism is a style of thought, based upon an ontological and epistemological distinction between the Orient and (most of the time) the Occident." Moreover, the author says that Orientalism has a political purpose "for dominating, restructuring and having authority over the Orient."

Bernard Lewis, in one of his most interesting papers, explained that there was a link between Western colonialism and the rise of Orientalism.[10] The Orientalists usually studied oriental history, religion and classics and became expert on oriental subjects. They also became interested in Islāmic history, and tried to interpret the history of the Islāmic *Ummah* (global Islāmic community) according to Western concepts and interests. A combination of motives (colonial, diplomatic, commercial and intellectual) provided incentives for Western powers to open centres of Oriental Studies at various colleges, universities and institutes. Gradually, Islāmic Studies in general and Islāmic history in particular were studied critically by many European professors and specialists, who gained well-deserved recognition for their outstanding contributions to different fields of Oriental Studies.

Lewis also explained that Orientalism may have begun as a colonial enterprise but it ended up on the academic agenda of a number of universities. Britain, France, Germany, Italy and Czarist Russia provided some of the oldest centres of Oriental Studies in Europe. For instance, France established *École Nationale des Langues Orientales Vivantes* in Paris in 1795 CE, to train interpreters for its Levant Service; it also trained officials for diplomatic and military service at a later date. This was the beginning of teaching of oriental languages such as Arabic, Turkish and Persian in France. Czar Alexander I of Russia (d. 1825 CE) founded a chair of oriental history and geography at the University of St. Petersburg in 1804 CE. This was followed by other Russian centres to teach Arabic, Turkish and Persian languages and even Islāmic history. The Southern part of Czarist Russia had a large Muslim population, hence chairs of Islāmic and Turkish studies were opened in many universities in the USSR during the twentieth century CE. There are now many chairs of Arabic and Middle Eastern Studies at the Universities of London, Oxford, Cambridge, Manchester, Exeter, St. Andrews and Edinburgh of Britain, Sorbonne in Paris, the University of Rome, the University of Leiden, and a large number of American universities such as Chicago, Harvard, Princeton, Los Angeles, Connecticut and Yale.

According to recent surveys on the subject by Albert Hourani (d. 1993 CE), Islāmic history is taught in at least twenty universities in Western Europe, twenty universities in North America and another twenty universities in the Middle East and North Africa.[11] There are at least thirty professors who can devote their full attention to Islāmic history in America; and another fifteen to twenty teachers each in Britain, France and Germany. Similar numbers are found in Turkey, Syria, Jordan, Egypt, Israel and so on.

Unfortunately, Hourani's report on Islāmic history does not take into account the status of Islāmic history in South Asian countries (with a Muslim population of nearly 400 million) such as Pakistan, India and Bangladesh, and the South-East Asian universities of Malaysia, Indonesia and Brunei Darussalam. There are at least forty professors and lecturers involved in teaching Islāmic history in those countries. However, Islāmic history in the Indian, Pakistani and Bangladeshi contexts not only includes the history of the caliphs and sultans of the Middle East but also the history of local and national Muslim dynasties. In South-East Asia, Islāmic history of the Middle East is taught in the Departments of Islāmic Studies of the University of Malaya, the Faculty of Islāmic Studies at the Universiti Kebangsaan Malaysia (National University of Malaysia) and in the Department of History of Brunei University. The emphasis of Islāmic history in South-East Asian countries is on the classical period of Islāmic history, from the era of the Prophet to the fall of the 'Abbasid Caliphate. The recent trend in history teaching in regional universities emphasises the history of the Association of the South-East Asian Nations (ASEAN). According to Professor Hourani's report, there are some two to three hundred teachers, lecturers and Professors of Islāmic history in the world, excluding

South and South-east Asian universities. I add to his figure at least forty more teaching Islāmic history at colleges and universities of Pakistan, Bangladesh, India, Malaysia, Indonesia, Brunei and so on. The total number of Islāmic historians today may be about 350. In spite of this, the state of Islāmic history is said to be at least a century behind the development of European history as an academic discipline. Islāmic history needs more full time researchers, teachers and professors to advance the subject to a higher standard of professionalism.

In the course of the twentieth century CE Western methods of historical research have been applied to the study of Islāmic history. Due to the involvement of Orientalists in the study of Islāmic history, there have been additions to the traditional sources of the subject. For instance, the traditional approach to the study of Islāmic history was to rely almost exclusively on the history books written by early Muslim historians. However, the situation is not the same now. The Islāmic historians trained by Orientalists have come to realise that the classical books on *ta'rīkh* are not adequate in themselves for the study of any period of Islāmic history. One has to take into account all the literary, geographical, religious and historical sources of any period to achieve a proper understanding of its history. Moreover, the Orientalists have emphasised that we should not rely on the written sources only, but must also study the 'other sources' of Islāmic history, among them the inscriptions written on stone and metal objects such as coins, medals, and other artefacts, and archival sources of all kinds including papyrus documents found in Egypt and elsewhere in the Middle East. Thus, an Islāmic historian today has to take into account numismatic evidence, archival records, epigraphic sources, contemporary diplomatic documents, which may have been preserved in countries outside the Middle East, unpublished manuscripts which may be preserved in any library in the world, and so on. In the case of Islāmic cities and monuments, new archaeological findings and reports have been made available recently to the Islāmic historian. There are also many new research tools for Islāmic history available today such as bibliographies including *Index Islamicus*, *Index Iranicus*, *Index Arabicus*, *Studies on early Islāmic papyri*, and all publications and sources covered in the book, *Historians of the Middle East*.[12] Islāmic history is emerging as a newly developed discipline. It is fair to say that the Orientalists have widened the scope of inquiry of Islāmic history. For instance, R. S. Humphreys has recently published a book entitled *Islāmic History: A framework for inquiry* which evaluates some significant modern writings on various aspects of the subject.

Muslims in general take the term Islāmic history for granted. Muslim intellectuals of former generations have never defined the subject or explained its content. Hence Islāmic history, like the concept of history itself, remains an undefined discipline. Although it is highly probable that Muslims in the past used the term *ta'rīkh* in the sense of Islāmic history, they also applied it to the general concept of history. However, the modern concept of Islāmic history, in the Orientalist sense, is something more than what the Muslims understood by *ta'rīkh*. The definition of Islāmic history today is a matter of some complexity. Hence R. S. Humphreys admits, "Islāmic history presents severe challenges even to an experienced specialist. Many of these are technical in nature, e.g. the multitude of languages needed to read both sources and modern scholarship, the vast number of major texts still in manuscript, the poor organisation of libraries and archives. More important, however, is the difficulty of grasping the subject as a whole, of developing the clear sense of the broad themes and concepts through which this sprawling and underdeveloped field of study can be bound together."[13] To understand the entire field of Islāmic history becomes an illusory goal. Although the Orientalists are nowadays much criticised and even demonised by some Arab scholars, such as 'Abd al-Laṭīf Tibāwī (d. 1981 CE) and Edward Said, their criticism is not specially focused on the field of Islāmic history. Therefore, the contributions of the Orientalists towards the expansion of the field of Islāmic history can still be seen as useful. The way Islāmic history is taught depends largely on the professional expertise of individual teachers and professors. This situation gives the professors an opportunity to plan their syllabus according to the personnel and their sources at the disposal of institutions. However, in the West, the term Islāmic history may be used to cover any one of the following: (i) the history of the early Islāmic preaching *(da'wah)* and the founding of the Islāmic State, the territorial conquests of the Muslims and the expansion of the Islāmic state of Madinah into an Islāmic empire under the rule of the *Khalīfahs*; (ii) the history of the Arabs after the advent of Islām and of the Middle Eastern states; (iii) the history of the Islāmic religion and the achievements of Muslims in the fields of science, philosophy and literature; and (iv) the general history of the Islāmic peoples as well as their beliefs and dominant institutions.[14] These are the four different approaches to Islāmic history in Western universities.

Recent writings on Islāmic history by Muslim writers from South Asia include: Abdul Hamid Siddiqui's (d. 1978 CE) *An Islāmic concept of history*[15]; Syed Ali Ashraf's *The Qur'ānic concept of History*[16]; Anis Ahmad's *Reorientation of Islāmic history*[17]; Ahmed Hasan Dani's *A Typology of Muslim Historiography* from the perspective of Islāmic philosophy of history[18]; and Qasim Hassan's *Some problems relating to the study of Islāmic civilisation.*[19]

All these essays were published during the last quarter of the twentieth century at a time when debates on Orientalism and Islāmic History were taking place elsewhere in the academia. Among these writers, Qasim Hassan, Anis Ahmad and Abdul Hamid Siddiqi were more involved in theology than history and their ideas of history are flawed, lacking in originality. Ahmed Hasan Dani and Syed Ali Ashraf, on the other hand, raised some points which are not directly relevant to Islāmic history although they subscribed to a philosophy of history of their own.

Ahmed Hasan Dani's statement on history is not only confusing but misleading in many respects. He says, "Thus from the Holy *Qur'ān* it is possible to derive the philosophy of history that can enlighten man in his effort to develop historical knowledge."[20] He is a well-known Muslim scholar who includes within the scope of his essay a brief reference to the 'creation myth', epistemology, eschatology and the travelogues of Abū Raiḥān al-Bīrūnī (d. 1051 CE) and Ibn Baṭṭūtah (d. 1369 CE), as well as the so-called 'geographical history' of *Kitāb al-Masālik wa'l-mamālik* by Ibn Khurdadhbih (d. 846 CE). It is hard to sympathise with the writer's superficial view of 'geographical history'; the 'road-books' *(Masālik)* are indeed sources for the study of economic geography of the 'Abbāsid Empire, but not any kind of 'geographical history' as he assumes. It would have been helpful if Ahmed Dani had studied the original Arabic sources of Islāmic history. I suspect that he has based his statement on an English translation of Ibn Khurdadhbih's 'road-book'. His philosophy of history was summed up in the following sentence: "The role of the individual in society is the deciding factor in history." Although Dani's statement is not original, still it is an echo of a certain idea of Aristotle (d. 322 BC) who allegedly said, "History is an account of what an individual human being has done and suffered",[21] yet Dani must be aware of the view of other historians that history is not primarily concerned with any individual life, but is more interested in the collective life of the community and public events in society. Moreover, it is generally held that the study of an individual life is essentially the subject-matter of biography and not of history. There are many Muslim scholars who have been misled by this so-called philosophy of history. In fact, the latest view on the subject is that such a philosophy of history is neither philosophy nor history.

Syed Ali Ashraf's seminar paper on *The Qur'ānic Concept of History* is an appreciation and recognition of Abdul Hamid Siddiqui's earlier work on the subject. Ali Ashraf emphasised two points. First, he thinks that history has an ethical purpose. Mankind should learn from the lessons of ancient nations which perished for violating God's message and spreading tyranny and injustice in human society. In fact, the history of a nation or nations may have many lessons for all of us. The Holy *Qur'ān* alludes to the history of many ancient peoples like Noah's folk, Lot's folk, Abraham's folk and the Ād, Thamūd,[22] etc. and reminds us about the fate of nations which were destroyed in the past for violating God's commandments and forgetting divine revelations. The rise and fall of nations depend on their moral standard as ordained by God. Thus history and morality are intertwined. But an attempt to teach history for the sole purpose of deducing moral lessons for mankind would be a change, if not novelty, in the teaching of history. It would result in a separate kind of history, which we could call ethicohistory. Such an approach would make history an adjunct to theology and metaphysics.

Secondly, he held an unusual view on the concept of time which is somehow linked with a theory of long-range periodisation of history. As far as periodisation is concerned he thinks that there are three broad periods in world history. The first period extends from God's creation of the prototypes of mankind in the shapes of Adam and Eve and their descendants to the era of the Prophet Muḥammad ﷺ. This ancient period of history covered the Prophets and patriarchs – from Adam to Muḥammad (including Noah, Moses, Abraham and Jesus, peace be upon them). This is a vast subject which was covered in the first nine volumes of the translation of the *History of al-Ṭabarī*. The second (middle) period of history, according to the same author, begins with the Righteous Caliphs *(Khulafā' al-Rāshidīn)* till the regeneration of mankind after the second coming of Jesus *('alaihi al-Salām)*. However, history only deals with the past and does not include the future. The third period will begin with mankind's gradual decline and downfall through loss of consciousness of spiritual and moral values, and the ultimate destruction of the entire creation by God. This part of periodisation is part of eschatology that is beyond the scope of history.

Periodisation or the division of history into specific periods is also an issue about which Muslim scholars are not quite sure of. Unlike the above theory, the periodisation of Islāmic history, in practice, begins with the life of the Prophet Muḥammad ﷺ, followed by the history of the *Khulafā' al-Rāshidīn*, followed by the Umayyads, 'Abbasids, Mamluks and Ottomans and their successor-states, etc. Such a division of Islāmic history into broad periods is essentially a dynastic approach[23] to history which assumes that personalities of rulers produced new characteristics in each period of history. Should we stick to this approach or change it to a cultural approach, or an area study approach? If the Muslim historians are serious about the future of Islāmic history as an academic discipline, they have to produce new discourse on the nature, objective, parameter and structure of Islāmic history. There is a need for much research and coordination of efforts among Muslim historians and various interested groups of academic scholars to promote Islāmic history as a subject of high standard and academic excellence.

As a conclusion to this discussion of Islāmic history as an academic discipline, it is necessary to consider the thought of some Muslim scholars of the twentieth century. Some believe that history is a source of nationalism. Their argument in favour of teaching history amounts to this: we need history as a source and justification for our nationalism. This attitude has affected not only the writings but also the teaching and interpretation of history in some Arab and Muslim countries where history is recast to cover the story of the nation-state. Nationalists have often idolised personalities or highlighted events in their national history with emotion and exaggeration. On the whole, nationalist historiography tends to favour a selective approach, recording some events of the nation's past and omitting others. Such an attitude is contrary to historical fact. Anwar G. Chejne (d. c. 1981 CE) drew the attention of his readers to the Syrian government's decree of 30

May 1947 CE regarding the purpose of teaching history: "to strengthen the nationalist and patriotic sentiments in the hearts of the people ... because the knowledge of the nation's past is one of the most important incentives to patriotic behaviour." However, nationalism is not compatible with the universal message of Islām. Islāmic history is essentially an international history of the Islāmic community *(Ummah)*. It is not conceived as an ethnic or racial history. This is one of the problems of the titles and interpretations of some books which, surprisingly, cover, partly or fully, the general field of Islāmic history, such as Syed Ameer Ali's (d. 1928 CE) *A short history of the Saracens*, P. K. Hitti's *History of the Arabs*, Bernard Lewis' summary of *The Arabs in History* and Albert Hourani's *A History of the Arab Peoples*. The authors of these books tend to make early Islāmic history an exclusively Arab affair. Demographically, the Arabs today hardly constitute 25% of all the Islāmic peoples.

On the other hand, there are few printed works that can effectively serve the purpose of textbooks of Islāmic history. Among the available books one could mention Carl Brockelmann's (d. 1956 CE) balanced introduction to Islāmic history, entitled *History of the Islāmic Peoples*, which gives a vivid account of the Islāmic community from the pre-Islāmic period till the post-Ottoman era. The author covered not only political history but also cultural life of the various Muslim communities. The work embodies some good features of Western scholarship on Islāmic history written before the Second World War. *The Venture of Islām: Conscience and History in a World Civilisation* is a three-volume study of Islāmic religious and cultural history by Marshall G. S. Hodgson (d. 1968 CE), an American Quaker historian. The author takes a sociological approach to the religious and cultural history of the Muslims. Finally, we may refer to the two volumes of *Islāmic History: A New Interpretation* by M. A. Shaban (d. 1992 CE). The author's claim to a 'new interpretation' of Islāmic history rests on his careful reading between the lines of the Arabic texts of the histories of Ṭabarī and Ibn al-Athīr, and also a refutation of misinterpretations by the Orientalists. By common consent, Shaban's first volume of *Islāmic History: A New Interpretation* (600 – 750 CE) (Cambridge University Press, 1971 CE) is, in many ways, the best one-volume introduction to early Islāmic history. The second volume of *Islāmic History: A New Interpretation* (750 – 1055 CE) covers early 'Abbāsid history till the end of the Buwayhid amirate and the Fāṭimid Khalifate. Although the second volume of Shaban's Islāmic history has new insights, it is not as original as the first volume. Among the twentieth century CE learned journals which have been well known for publishing research articles on Islāmic history, we should mention the *Islāmic Culture* (1927 – 1995 CE) published by the Dā'irat al-Ma'ārif al-Osmania, in Hyderabad Deccan, Andhra Pradesh, India. The latest edition of the *Encyclopaedia of Islām* which is being published (1960 – 1996 CE) (eight volumes in print) by E. J. Brill, Leiden, is also an important reference work for the study of Islāmic history and civilisation. It publishes short scholarly articles written by Orientalists as well as Muslim contributors covering the entire period of Islāmic history.

I was impressed by a statement issued by the modern Turkish historian, Halil Inalcik, about the merit of Islāmic history as a unifying factor of the *Ummah*. He wrote in 1953, "In my opinion, historical studies will form a strong foundation for the real cultural movements in Islāmic countries today. The objective study of Islāmic history with Western methodology will bring about general progress in all Islāmic learning. Certain Islāmic fundamentals such as the *Qur'ān*, *Sharī'ah*, and the Islāmic institutions have provided the unity of Islām's history and have played a role as the most important factor throughout the history of all Islāmic peoples. Thus, the history of any one Islāmic country cannot be understood unless it is studied in the general framework of Islāmic history."[24]

This is indeed a very interesting view of the role of Islāmic history within the broader context of the Islāmic community. It will probably be respected for years. But there is a problem which may prevent Muslims of different backgrounds from accepting this view in its entirety. The idea of accepting Western epistemology unreservedly is a sensitive issue for conservative Muslims. Inalcik's suggestion that we study Islāmic history according to Western methodology will not be easy to swallow for many Islāmic historians, for those who would like to teach Islāmic history within the framework of Islāmic epistemology. Muslims may continue to resist any suggestion of accepting Western methodology in the pursuit of Islāmic history. The satisfactory resolution of this thorny issue may have to be left in the hands of the next generation of Islāmic historians.

It is essential for Islāmic historians to have a clear perception[25] of their subject, and to contribute towards teaching as well as research. Islāmic history binds and links the different segments of the entire Islāmic community to a common origin and heritage. All the nation-states of Muslims have their local and national history, but their identity as Muslims is rooted in Islāmic history. At some point in history Islām came to different parts of the Muslim world either through military conquests by Arabs, Persians, Turks, Berbers, Indians[26] and the Malays and other ethnic groups of Muslims, or through proselytisation by Muslim missionaries, preachers and emigrants. Islāmic history is like a thread that weaves all parts of the *Ummah* into a tapestry. As *Allāh* has beautifully said, Muslims are like a 'solid structure'.[27] The different parts of the Islāmic *Ummah*, the global Muslim community, are like bricks in that structure. Islāmic history is the collective memory of all the Muslim nations and groups. It is the record of our civilisation. Muslims should preserve the sources of their history and constantly add new chapters to it with objectivity and impartiality.

The historian Ibn al-Athīr[28] recognised many benefits, this worldly as well as otherworldly, to be derived from reading history. It reminded the people about the past and the transitoriness of human life. It provided examples of good rulers who were praised and wicked kings who were despised and condemned. History demonstrated the consequences of tyranny which ruined countries and civilisations, inflicting sufferings to people and causing losses of lives and property and perpetuating injustice and conflicts. History also supplies beneficial experiences from the past of mankind, and enriches human intellect and wisdom. Thus history teaches by past examples of individuals and nations. On the other hand, the goal of history, according to the Muslim scholar al-Sakhawī, is to seek God's kindness through good deeds. This is an indication of the serious intent and sacred duty of Muslim historians to investigate and record the truth, without bias or prejudice, regarding the affairs of humankind. This altruistic concept of 'the goal of history' originated in the Islāmic civilisation only a generation or so after the death of the great Muslim historian Ibn Khaldūn who wrote a cyclical theory of history and the concept of group solidarity *('aṣabīyah)*. Islāmic history mirrors the past of the Islāmic community and points to the right course of action, knowing the pitfalls of our forebears to avoid disasters and catastrophes, to pursue the right course of action along the straight path and thus ensure our survivial with dignity, achieving success and triumphs.

References

1. 'Abd al-'Azīz al-Dūrī, *Baḥth fī nash'at 'Ilm al-ta'rīkh 'ind al-'Arab (Nuṣūṣ wa-durūs) al-Maṭba'ah al-Kathulikiyah*, Beirut, Lebanon, 1960 CE, pp. 13-102. Cf. an English translation of this book as *The Rise of Historical Writing among the Arabs* by L. I. Conrad, Princeton University Press, Princeton, New Jersey, USA, 1983 CE, pp. 3-159. Cf. also A. A. Duri, 'The Iraqi School of History to the Ninth Century – A Sketch', in *Historians of the Middle East* edited by B. Lewis and P. M. Holt, London, UK, 1962 CE, pp.46-53.
2. Shams al-Dīn Muḥammad ibn 'Abd al-Raḥmān Al-Sakhawī, *Al-I'lān bi'l-tawbikh li-man dhamma al-ta'rīkh*, Damascus, Syria 1930 CE, p.45.

3. *Ibid.*, pp. 6; 78-81. Cf. Ibn al-Athīr, *al-Kāmil fil-Ta'rīkh*, Beirut, Lebanon, 1967 CE, pp. 9-10. Cf. also Muhammad Abdul Jabbar Beg, *Wisdom of Islāmic Civilization*, University of Malaya Press, Kuala Lumpur, Malaysia, 1980 CE, pp.61-62; idem, Fourth edition, Kuala Lumpur, Malaysia, 1986 CE; pp.85-86.
4. Al-Sakhawī's book, *Al-I'lān bi'l-tawbīkh li-man dhamma al-Ta'rīkh* on the sources of Islāmic historical literature was edited from a manuscript in the collection of Ahmad Taymur Pasha. It was published by al-Mat'ba'ah al-Taraqqi, Damascus, Syria, in 1930 CE. The Arabic book contains 174 printed pages and is available in English translation by Professor F. Rosenthal.
5. Franz Rosenthal, *A History of Muslim Historiography*, E. J. Brill, Leiden, The Netherlands, 1968 CE, p.15.
6. *Ibid.*, p. 531.
7. R. S. Humphreys, 'Qur'anic myth and narrative structure in early Islāmic Historiography', in F. M. Clover et al (eds.), *Tradition and Innovation in Late Antiquity*, The University of Wisconsin Press, Wisconsin, USA, 1989 CE, p. 281.
8. *The History of Al-Ṭabarī*, divided into 38 volumes, is being published by The State University of New York (SUNY), Albany, New York, USA, under the General Editor Ehsan Yar-Shater in the Bibliotheca Persica since 1985 CE. Three of the thirty-eight volumes were published in 1985. Many other translated volumes have been published since. Volumes i-ix cover from Creation to the ancient history of the Kingdoms, Prophets and Patriarchs including Prophet Muḥammad ﷺ.
9. Edward Said, *Orientalism*, p. 2.
10. Bernard Lewis, *Approaches to Islāmic History in Europe and America* (offprint of a Conference held in Belgium, 11-14 September 1961 CE), Brussels, Belgium, 1962 CE, pp. 1-12.
11. Albert Hourani, 'The present state of Islāmic and Middle Eastern historiography', in *Europe and the Middle East*, London, UK, 1980 CE, pp. 162-63. A. Hourani, (Chapter 3) History, in L. Binder (ed.), *The Study of the Middle East*, New York, USA, 1976 CE, pp. 97-135.
12. B. Lewis and Holt (eds.), *Historians of the Middle East*, Oxford University Press, London, UK, 1962 CE, pp. 503.
13. R. S. Humphreys, *Islāmic History: A Framework for Inquiry*, Revised ed., London, UK, 1991 CE, p. ix.
14. Ira P. Lapidus, 'Islām and the historical experience of the Muslim peoples', in E. M. Kerr (ed.), *Islāmic Studies: A Tradition and its Problems*, California, USA, 1980 CE, p. 89.
15. Abdul Hamid Siddiqui, 'An Islāmic concept of history', in I. R. Faruqi, Abdullah Omar Naseef (eds.), *Social and Natural Sciences*, (Islāmic Education Series, General Editor Syed Ali Ashraf), Hodder and Stoughton, London, UK, c. 1980 CE, p. 41.
16. Syed Ali Ashraf, *The Qur'ānic Concept of History*, Seminar Papers 4, The Islāmic Foundation, Leicester, UK, 1980 CE, pp. 8-12.
17. Anis Ahmad, 'Reorientation of Islāmic History: some methodological issues' in *Islām: Source and Purpose of Knowledge*, published by International Institute of Islāmic Thought (IIIT), Virginia, USA, 1988 CE, p. 287.
18. Ahmed Hasan Dani, 'A Typology of Muslim historiography from the perspective of Islāmic philosophy of history', in Islām*: Source and Purpose of Knowledge*, Islāmisation of Knowledge series, no. 5, IIIT, Virginia, USA, 1988 CE, p. 318.
19. Qasim Hassan, 'Some problems relating to the study of Islāmic civilisation', in *Bulletin of the Institute of Islāmic Studies*, Aligarh Muslim University, No.4, 1960 CE, p. 17.
20. *Op. cit.*, pp. 318, 323.
21. Isaiah Berlin, quoted in *History and Theory*, The Hague, The Netherlands, 1961 CE, p. 1.
22. *Al-Qur'ān*, chapter 22, verses 42-47. Cf. Hajj Ta'lim Ali/Thomas B. Irving (Translator), *The Noble Qur'ān: Arabic text and English Translation*, Amana Books, Brattleboro, Vermont, USA, p. 337.
23. M. Morony, '*Bayn al-Fitnatayn*: Problems in the Periodisation of Early Islāmic History', in *Journal of Near Eastern Studies*, vol. 40, no. 3, 1981 CE, pp. 247-251.
24. Halil Inalcik, 'Some remarks on the study of history in Islāmic countries', *The Middle East Journal*, vol. 7, no. 4, Autumn, Washington DC, USA, 1953 CE, p. 455.
25. Muhammad Abdul Jabbar Beg, 'Perceptions of history in Western and Islāmic education', in *Islāmic University (Quarterly Academic Journal)*, edited by S. M. A. Shahrastani *et al*, Verdun, Beirut, Lebanon (published by the International College of Islāmic Sciences, Kilburn, London), vol. i, no. 1, 1994 CE, pp. 53-61.
26. By the word 'Indians' the author denotes the Indian rulers such as the Sultans of Delhi, Padishahs (Moghal Badshahs) and Nawabs of the Indian subcontinent in the pre-modern period.
27. *Al-Qur'ān*, chapter 61, verse4.
28. Ibn al-Athir, *Al-Kāmil fi'l-ta'rīkh*, Beirut, Lebanon, 1967 CE, vol. i, pp. 7-9.

A Programme for Muslim Education in a Non-Muslim Society

Sahib Mustaqim Bleher

Any programme for Muslim education in a non-Muslim society, irrespective of regional or circumstantial variations, needs to address two basic questions: Firstly, what are the specific aspects of Muslim education, both in terms of values of contents and methodology, missing from the education programmes available in the environment of a non-Muslim society? Or, from the reverse point of view, what are the weaknesses of the prevailing non-Muslim education programmes which are overcome or, better still, avoided in a Muslim education programme? Secondly, after contrasting these two streams of education programmes, what are the obstacles involved in carrying out Muslim education, and are these obstacles affecting some aspects of a Muslim education programme more than others?

Most programmes of Muslim education in non-Muslim societies have been of a remedial nature and this has been the cause of their all too obvious limitations. Muslims faced with problems or difficulties have responded by searching for ways of redress, often without a clear vision of what they ultimately want to achieve. Doctoring the symptoms has been the standard approach of Muslims in the West and education is no exception. The underlying reason is that immigrant Muslims arrived with the intention to improve their social and economic situation through a temporary stay in an alien environment; their favourite response to education problems – if taken seriously at all - was to insist on the preservation of traditions brought with them from 'back home'. Such a short-term and backward-looking approach was harmful more than helpful, and it has surely hampered the progress of a younger generation who, instead of being at the forefront of the introduction of Islāmic principles into non-Muslim society, have either lost part of their Muslim identity in order to gain worldly opportunities or *vice-versa*. There are, no doubt, notable exceptions but this article is more concerned with the general trend than individual cases.

To permit long-term planning for Muslim education in a non-Muslim environment, in which an immigrant Muslim population has long-since been transformed into a settled community, it is necessary to tackle the subject from the roots. Only by doing this can we gain an understanding and vision that will ensure a resultant education programme will achieve the permanence of Islām in non-Muslim societies; this must be the ultimate aim of our endeavours. The centre-piece of a Muslim education programme, therefore, has to be the worldview of Islām and the place of man therein. In Islām, it being a faith-based ideology of Divine origin, everything focuses on the Divine element which is always part of every situation.[1] This differs greatly from a secular worldview within which man is the master of his own fortune, free to use his abilities as he pleases, for better or for worse. Christianity, by having God resting on the seventh day, is, in theory, a Divine understanding of the world in which we live. In practice, however, it is much closer to the secular interpretation of events. In the Divine environment of Islām, man's freedom is restricted not only by the freedom of other men but also by a sense of purpose in his actions. Islām'*s* approach to life situations is, therefore, harmonious and synthetic, fitting in with the created world in contrast to the secular, synthetic approach of dissecting, controlling and possessing which, instead of enhancing the good in creation, has an ultimately destructive tendency. Hence, in Islām fundamentalism is a positive concept, because the original foundations are good, being of Divine origin, whereas in the secular philosophy the upholding of fundamentals is regarded as a hindrance to innovation which is a tool in the competition for supremacy.

The holistic approach of Islām represents the first major concept in Muslim education which is not found in non-Muslim educational programmes. The secular education model cannot do justice to the human beings it serves to educate, because it deals with various aspects of human nature in a fragmented way, ignoring their inter-relationships and denying the Divine origin of them all. Man is far more complex than to justify a reduction of the educational process to the cognitive element alone. The human being consists of a body, soul and mind and has understanding, feeling, character and patterns of behaviour. Any education programme which concentrates unduly on the cognitive aspects of the mind and neglects any or all of the other faculties to a lesser or greater degree will result in an adult who is markedly imbalanced; modern civilisation is ample proof of that.

This leads us to another key difference between Muslim and non-Muslim education: The former is geared-up to the perfection of the individual human being and the society of those individuals, solely for the pleasure of *Allāh*. Non-Muslim education is merely concerned with the usefulness of certain abilities which can be developed in a given context. In other words, in a secular education programme the human being, having been denied his Divine origin, is being dehumanised and mechanised into a subservient tool of temporary man-made processes which regulate his life more rigidly than any natural or religious law. Consequently, for the appointment of any member of society to a position of leadership and responsibility, professional specialisation is far more relevant than moral qualification.

The paragraphs above have described the environmental context within which a Muslim education programme operates and the purpose of such a programme. A third feature has to be the contents of the programme itself.

Knowledge in Islām has two branches: absolute knowledge based on revelation, and cognitive acquired knowledge ('the sciences' in the limited modern secular sense). Revealed knowledge, which has its own branches of study (the *Qur'ān*, *Sunnah*, *Sīrah*, *Fiqh* and *Usūl al-Fiqh* and *Lughah*), is missing entirely from the non-Muslim education programme. The acquired knowledge which branches off into natural, intellectual, imaginative, practical and applied sciences, is being taught without an understanding of the relevance of each to the other and to humanity at large. It was the contents of the school curriculum which was recognised by Muslims in the West as a problem, together with the 'hidden curriculum' which resulted in behaviour by their children which they were not altogether too happy about.

Having thus outlined, in brief, the basic aspects that a Muslim education programme needs to take account of, what are the obstacles faced when trying to develop a Muslim education programme in a non-Muslim society and putting it into practice?

Given that the above description reflects the truth adequately, our first and greatest obstacle is not, as is popularly supposed, a lack of money, but our own lack of understanding and an improper attitude. As a Muslim community in the heartland of secularism we lack awareness of the underlying realities and display an essentially secular approach cloaked in Islāmic garments. This having been our approach in so many spheres of life, of which education is but one (albeit one of the utmost importance), it comes as no surprise to see that we have had, on the whole, more failure than success in the Islāmisation of our environment. What is meant by 'secular' in this challenging statement is the absence of thorough devotion while we continue to give unmaintainable structures a glossy veneer to show our 'achievements' to the outside world. We could call it 'the Hollywood syndrome'; all show and no substance. We hope and pray that nobody shall see the emptiness behind the pretence of a shiny facade. In old Islāmic art, when working on the ornamentation of sacred buildings, the artist would produce his best work in a corner least accessible to the public eye so as to escape the praise of the observer; thus his work was perfected for the praise of *Allāh* alone. This was the artist's charity, his chance for pure devotion, the sense of which we have lost, producing instead half-baked expressions for short-lived public consumption. We have succumbed to reprogramming as our attitude has been taken over by secular impressiveness; our work mirrors this metamorphosis. The result of our efforts no longer stands the test of time; little wonder, then, that it fails to convince. How, therefore, can we be so foolishly vain to believe that our work will ignite the revolution against secularism when, in fact, we are copying it day after day?

Pretence has become a common feature in the field of Muslim education in the West today. Underachievement in Muslim schools is blamed on a lack of support from a non-Muslim government. Does Islām only survive when it is supported by its antagonists? Muslim girls' schools are seen as an ideal opportunity to improve the girls' marriage prospects by way of guaranteeing her chastity, rather than as a means to equip young Muslim women with an understanding of a path through life which she will never lose. Parents are happy to off-load their responsibilities for the Islāmic education of their children to the local weekend school without showing any willingness to make greater sacrifices themselves or, at least, to adjust their lifestyles to provide a more Islāmic atmosphere at home. On the whole, we have reduced Islām to a religion in the secular sense while insisting in debate with non-Muslims that it is a complete way of life. Our mosques are still full on special occasions but they are no longer the property nor the expression of a thriving Muslim community.

It could even be said that the Muslim community no longer exists as such. It is stricken with fever and needs respiratory help itself, instead of being able to provide the support any family unit needs whilst trying desperately to hold on to Islām. The increase in family break-ups amongst Muslims, although still moderate in comparison to the rest of society, is a symptom of this painful reality. Isolation is the greatest obstacle to an Islāmic lifestyle today. People who try to opt-out of the rat race of pointless materialism soon find themselves pushed into a corner.

Imagine yourself as the parent of young children imprisoned in a council house without a garden in a run-down inner-city district. The outside world is a raging monster waiting to eat up your children. There are no uncles or aunts living across the road you can send them to, something which would allow the children to see that Islām extends beyond your imagination (as well as giving you a rest from endless childish questions, quarrels and problems!). You send them to school and they come back as enemies who despise you and regard you as ignorant and a hindrance to ambitions their friends and teachers have put into their heads. You send them to Islāmic classes and the teacher beats Islām out of them or contradicts everything you have taught them about Islām. You send them to play with the children of your Muslim friends – not the lapsed, careless Muslim, but the good, active one who works so hard to spread Islām that he neglects his own family – and you get them back with a belly full of *Ḥaram* sweets and a head full of super-hero comics and computer games. You try to take them on holiday to a Muslim country, to perform *Ḥajj* or *'Umrah* perhaps, and all they will learn (assuming they remember all that you have taught them, for example that cleanliness is an integral part of faith) is that Muslims have become bereft of faith. Faced with such a situation how on earth are you going to make them understand that Islām is supreme, the best...?

The obstacles to overcome whilst attempting to establish a Muslim programme of education are, therefore, more complex and more basic than we often wish to admit, and it is for that reason that a strategy of protection, of trying to keep our children away from bad influences, cannot work. Teaching Islām in a non-Muslim environment is essentially confrontational. The aim must be to equip our children with sufficient knowledge, character, stability, experience and support to come out on top in this confrontation.

From the earliest possible age the teaching has to be consistent, regular and systematic to achieve this aim. Children have to acquire confidence in *Allāh* as Someone Who will never let them down; confidence in the home as a place of security and confidence in their own ability to face up to any struggle. This confidence has to be put to the test again and again. There has to be success and failure and it has to be followed up by the parents and educators so that the child benefits from the experience. It is essential, when selecting real-life situations for follow-up interpretation and analysis, for there to be more success stories than failures so that the child is not prone to give up when things turn sour. In a society which, in the main, has deviated from the right path, a child has to learn to consider being different from many of their peers as a positive quality. Any attempt to help them assimilate and fit in with the crowd will subsequently impair their ability to assert themselves as conscious Muslims; whilst such efforts may be originally intended to minimise the hurt of early conflict, this will lead to lasting pain through the loss of a distinct identity. The feeling of not wanting your child to 'lose out' is utterly misplaced whilst at the same time you want him or her to be somebody who will 'change it all': you cannot change something of which you are an integral part and which, in turn, is an integral part of yourself.

It should not be difficult to realise from all of this that the child's early years are the most important, and that the preoccupation of Muslim communities in Britain with arrangements for secondary and further education is somewhat misguided. The emphasis ought to be on building good foundations. To undo the negative influences already affecting the personality of young adults is a very difficult task. Attempting to protect young people at the age of puberty from both society and themselves is, therefore, unlikely to be successful. In contrast, a properly developed Islāmic personality will only need a little extra help to cope with the challenges of the secular way of life. We cannot, of course, shadow human beings forever (not that this would be desirable even if we could), so pre-school and primary education has to become the focus of our efforts. It is an additional 'plus' that organised education at this stage of life is easier to arrange and more affordable.

The aim ought to be to install certain essential concepts within the personality of the child such that they become an integral part of his or her being. To fill children's heads with Islāmic knowledge in the sense of historic and factual information is of secondary importance. Whilst the main concepts of Islām cannot be separated entirely from this information, it is readily available in books and the child or young adult can acquire it at any stage. As a community, our deficiency is not so much one caused by a lack of knowledge (even though this may well be apparently so) but by a lack of understanding and the ability to form a sense of judgement. What is needed, therefore, is much more of an Islāmic socialisation process, rather than simply Islāmic teaching.

The key concept is that of *Taqwā*, the awareness of *Allāh's* presence and the continuous responsibility we have towards Him in everything we do. To be able to reach the right conclusions, the children need to understand the chain of command or authority in Islām, where their actions are determined by the rules originating from *Allāh*, conveyed by the Prophet ﷺ and passed down and interpreted by the learned and elders. They need to understand that this third element in the chain, though demanding respect, can be challenged, but only on the basis of knowledge from the original sources. Alongside the awareness of *Allāh* and the relevance of His decrees for all of life's situations, the children need to have a proper awareness of themselves and their relationship with Allāh and the people surrounding them, past and present. Self-confidence has to be coupled with an ability for self-criticism, as the inability to accept criticism reflects an uncertainty of belief which leads to fanaticism. The most ardent dogmatic supporters of Islām have often signalled that their own convictions are weak simply by their inability to counter criticism with calm and reason. Children, therefore, have to be trained in the skills of intellectual argument as well as patience and tolerance. They have to understand that questions and doubts, even disbelief, do not necessarily constitute an attack against their faith but are a result of ignorance. They have to learn to adapt the methods of argument to the prospective outcome. An awareness of *what* can be achieved needs to precede a decision over *how* it can be achieved and any progress then made needs to be monitored constantly.

These are lofty aims because they mean that our children need not only to be good Muslims but also, as they live in a predominantly non-Muslim society, they need to understand the way a non-Muslim thinks without being fooled by his superimposed logic. They need to be trained in the art of dialectics without being confined by its limitations. For example, they need to be sure that interest decreases wealth and charity increases it, notwithstanding the apparent contradiction of immediate mathematical calculation. They, therefore, must be able to express and reaffirm their faith in the truths known to them *and* prove their validity by way of empirical evidence within the wider economy and the repercussions upon the individual where the saver, having gained a few pennies in interest, will have lost pounds in ensuing inflation and debt taxation.

Are we ever likely to achieve such heights of human perfection? Is it not all we can do to hold on to the main rituals and cultural expressions of Islām, to carve a niche for survival? This indeed is the key question. Are we going to foster an inward-looking or an outward-looking attitude? Are we, as Muslims, standard-bearers and an example for others, witnesses for mankind[2] who order what is good and forbid what is wrong[3], who care more for others (and that includes the disbelievers who depend on our guidance) than we care for ourselves, even if we are in hardship?[4] Or are we content to remain a ghettoised minority as long as we are given certain privileges which permit us to live in accordance with our own way of life? Is there Islām without *jihād*, the endless, restless struggle for betterment? Is there any prophet of *Allāh* (peace be upon them all) who claimed simply to have been sent to look after just himself and those who follow him? Can faith be separated from action? Can religion be separated from worldly affairs? Can justice be selective? Can a Muslim turn a blind eye to what is happening around him and still be a Muslim? The answers to all these questions are known to anybody whose conscience has not yet died. The question, therefore, is this: can we still prove worthy of having been chosen for *Allāh's* guidance?

Finally, we come back to the point about the right environment. We are rightly concerned that the environment of a non-Muslim society presents a negative influence upon our children. This is, however, only true in the absence of Islām as a living reality. The struggle of Muslims, even though in total isolation, to change this environment; the total devotion to live Islām, whatever the obstacles; the altruism of making the benefits of Islām available to everybody, whatever the criticisms; the life of *jihād* in the way of *Allāh*; the complete sacrifice of all personal, selfish ambitions to this cause; all provide the ideal training to impress upon a growing young Muslim. If we can get our children to be part of this, if they catch on, there is nothing in the world that can ever turn them away from Islām thereafter. First, though, before we sit back complacently to watch *The Message* on video, intending to give our children some Islāmic exposure, we have to live it ourselves. If the children are to take it seriously, the environment has to be real.

1. *Al-Qur'ān*, chapter 57, verse 4; chapter 58, verse 7.
2. *Ibid.*, chapter 2: verse 143.
3. *Ibid.*, chapter 3: verse 110.
4. *Ibid.*, chapter 59: verse 9.

Multicultural Education: an Islāmic perspective

Muhammad Ibrahim

History testifies to mankind's horrific potential to destroy itself. There have been many grotesque examples illustrating intolerance based on ignorance: the infamous Spanish Inquisition; the anti-Semitism of Christopher Columbus; the persecution of 'heathens' (including Jews and Muslims) in the name of Roman Catholicism; and the Nazi desire to create a 'master race' in Germany based on pagan values. Today, there are problems in Northern Ireland, the Middle East, India, Bosnia, and so on. It is hardly surprising, therefore, that religion is blamed for troubles across the world.

Unfortunately, ignorance continues to prevail. Just as it was easy to blame the Jews for the economic troubles in Nazi Germany of the thirties, so too it is easy to blame religion as the cause of so much suffering. Indeed, today we see a new 'scapegoat' emerging – the rise of 'Islāmophobia'. Much of the bigotry that leads people to condemn religion still exists. A Roman Catholic Cardinal, quoted some few years ago giving his response to a series of Religious Education (RE) textbooks, reportedly said, "It generates a falsely rosy picture of inter-religious relations." He went on, "The Divinity of Christ is only hinted at, the term Son of God is mentioned but left unexplained and the fact that Jesus is the only saviour and Redeemer of the human race is omitted." In fact, this series of text books has much to commend it and is a credit, in particular to those Catholics who were instrumental in its development. It clearly states in the foreword of its 'Teacher's Book': 'While [the series] draws principally on Catholic tradition it is open to any school community and to the religious traditions to which this may relate.' Indeed if it had fulfilled the wishes of the Cardinal it would have failed to meet its clearly stated objectives.

Such comments cause concern. For too long religion has been labelled as negative, so much so that there is considerable prejudice against its study as a subject. This is reflected in its demise in society generally, its gradual 'elimination' from the school curriculum, and the subsequent need for the 1988 Education Reform Act (ERA) to try to preserve its place in schools. One has to question the motives of the ERA. Is it really concerned about preserving the importance of religion? Or are the concerns of a small group of Christians paramount?

There are principally three motive for teaching RE in schools: the political, the religious and the educational. The political is largely concerned with maintaining the 'status quo', trying to revive the 'good old days'; the religious attempts to indoctrinate a particular faith; and the educational tries to ensure pupils are provided with the skills to make the most of their adult life as law abiding citizens. It is clear that the two former motives are doomed to fail as they are missing the real target of education – to educate!

I suggest that it is possible to present religion positively; encouraging people to think about religion favourably will help to create a more harmonious society. I am not saying that it will solve the problems of the world, but it will certainly go much further than the path of bigotry and intolerance. However, it is also important to recognise that religion by its nature deals with belief. Belief can be fundamentally divisive. It is therefore essential that we do not look just at the positive aspects, but also the tensions and divisions these differences cause. What we need to do is to learn how to cope with these differences; to learn how to set those essential guidelines necessary for people to live peacefully within a pluralistic society.

The second of the Cardinals's comments demonstrates another problem. We live in an age when we are all, children and adults alike, encouraged to question our beliefs and actions. Gone are the days of strict dogma, replaced now by healthy questioning and reappraisal of life stances. Gone also are the days when pupils were expected simply to accept and believe. Adolescents, in particular, are astute; they see beyond bigotry. It is not surprising, therefore, to find approaches like the Cardinal's rejected by so many youngsters. Today's youth want and deserve a meaningful education, in the sense that they want to see a purpose and a value to it. They are entitled to this, as it does, after all, involve their lives. Pupils have 'voted with their feet' against the dogmatic approach to RE; to expect all pupils in a multicultural society to believe 'the fact that Jesus is the only saviour' is to belittle them. I do not deny the right of Christians to believe such a statement; but I do object to the blind belief that they have the right to impose it on others – this could only be bigotry.

My intention is not to robe bigoted attitudes to religion, but to re-examine the role religion can play in creating a more harmonious and peaceful society. I shall of course focus on Islām as a means of conveying a fresh insight into the values of multicultural education and the lessons to be learnt from it.

The growth of Islām in Britain provokes mixed feelings. Some welcome it, others detest it, whilst many fall between the two. It is, therefore, difficult for someone not acquainted with Islām to acquire an objective view; it is not surprising to find people with mixed feelings. The art of educating is firstly to understand the position of the one being educated, and to move on from there. When approaching someone with superficial knowledge one might inadvertently promote rather than remove prejudice. This is, of course, one of the well-known dangers of what is referred to as 'tokenism' in education. An example would be devising a curriculum in which Christianity predominates, with only token lessons covering the other world faiths. Rather than educating it reinforces stereotypes. This is a danger in any top-heavy curriculum: instead of encompassing a healthy breadth of content, it breeds unhealthy narrowness, hardly useful for tomorrow's adult citizens.

It is important to realise that it is difficult for someone to be objective when they have been raised with a narrow viewpoint. It is easy to become condescending. Unfortunately, the attitude that only Christians will go to paradise whilst all others go to hell prevails. This attitude led to the persecution of non-Christians in the past. This is why I am deeply concerned by the above-mentioned remarks by a leading church figure such as the Cardinal. It is necessary to appreciate that attempts at solutions have been made by well-intentioned people from within this framework. This is why, all too often, we see other faiths being stamped with a Christian interpretation. It should be noted that many solutions and ideologies fail because they are based on narrow-minded ideals.

Looking back at the 1950s and 60s, we can see the beginnings of assimilation, combined with a growing realisation that people with different beliefs and cultural values were in Britain. Giddens describes assimilation as "the acceptance of a minority group by a majority population, in which the group takes over the values and norms of the dominant culture."[1] Put simply, this means, 'When in Rome, do as the Romans do.' It is a one-way process whereby the minority group is expected to adapt to and adopt the culture of the majority. The assumption is that the majority culture is superior and that there can be no exchange or sharing of values between cultures; one cannot enrich the other. This surely is the sort of intolerance that breeds racism. Unless there is willingness to accept change on the part of the minority, there must be a degree of compulsion.

Assimilation denies the fact that religion often crosses racial boundaries; it is a common assumption, for example, that in Britain all Muslims are Asians, whereas Islām is to be found all over the world and is firmly established here in Britain.

Roy Todd writes: "Some people who migrated to Britain in the 1960s argue that their children will not submit to some of the racism which they suffered and instead will challenge whatever hostility they encounter."[2] His interpretation is realistic and this is exactly what happens with Islām; hostility towards Islām will always be challenged. A subtle point is being made here: Islām is not aggressive but it is defensive; it will not cause hostility but will certainly defend itself when attacked.

At this point it should be made clear that there is often a difference between what Islām says and what Muslims do, despite the fact that (unlike Christianity) there is clear guidance on virtually every aspect of life in the *Qur'ān* and the example *(Sunnah)* of Prophet Muḥammad ﷺ. Muslims are called to follow the path of *Allāh*, as shown in the *Qur'ān* and the *Sunnah*:

> *O you who believe!*
> *Obey Allāh,*
> *and obey the Messenger,*
> *and those charged with authority among you.*
> *If you differ in anything among yourselves,*
> *refer it to Allāh and His Messenger,*
> *if you do believe in Allāh and the Last Day:*
> *that is best, and most suitable for final determination.*[3]

It is important to appreciate that there are certain values and norms from which Islām will not deviate (even if some 'Muslims' do), and it cannot be adapted or altered to any practice contrary to its basic teachings. In other words, Islām cannot be assimilated. Indeed, since Islām has so much that is morally superior to non-Islāmic practices prevalent in this society, I believe that in due course it is more likely that the majority culture will be assimilated within Islām (as has happened in Islāmic history).

Another approach for Muslims in Britain is separatism, defined as the encapsulation of minority cultures; withdrawal of minority groups; self-help and separate provision.

This approach is interesting and will probably be upheld by those wishing to have voluntary aided Muslim schools. They have a strong argument, and it is disconcerting to see the Government clearly operating double standards. It is the legal right of Muslims to apply for voluntary aided status for their schools. The strongly-held view is that the education system must be fair: either voluntary aided status is allowed for everybody, or it isn't granted to anybody. The double standards come into the picture when aided status is allowed for some groups but not others, even though the latter are also taxpayers and citizens deserving equality. How can it be right for voluntary aided status to be granted to Jewish schools, in some cases before they had even opened their doors, whilst operational Muslim schools, fulfilling all the educational criteria for voluntary aid, find the official goal posts being moved continuously?

Islām, by its very nature, is separatist. Indeed, all faith communities are; beliefs do separate people and it is necessary to appreciate this. Encouragimg greater autonomy for faith groups will lead to more harmony in society, not, as some people believe, the opposite. That this is so can be seen from the family unit, for example, which has proved time and time again to be the best foundation for a productive society. For the family group to work well it needs to have the freedom and privacy to operate at its own discretion. It is somewhat belittling to assume that any given community is incapable of governing its own affairs simply because it does not agree with all of the values of what is, as demonstrated above, an inadequate democratic structure.

It should also be borne in mind that religious values, per se, generally unite various groups against godlessness rather than divide them. The separatist approach has a lot to offer and deserves greater study instead of being summarily dismissed.

Another interesting approach is pluralism. Unfortunately, I have encountered Muslims who are too narrow in their understanding of what needs to be done in this respect.

Whilst some may advocate separatism and others pluralism, I suggest that we need both. In an ideal situation separatism would be the only viable system, but we do not live in an ideal world, so we must be pragmatic. There is a clear demand and need for 'separate' Muslim schools; the Muslim community's desire for these schools should be respected. Yet we recognise that they can only cater for a small percentage of the Muslim population. There will be many Muslims who, for one reason or another, will prefer instead the local state 'secular' (for want of a better word) school. Their children also have religious needs which must be met, and pluralism can provide a solution.

In presenting the case for pluralism, there needs to be a clear understanding of what it is, as there tend to be many definitions depending on whether the word is applied to economics, politics or education, etc.

Giddens defines pluralism as, "a society in which several ethnic groupings co-exist, each living in communities or regions largely separate from the others."[4] This is an interesting definition as it begs the readers to rack their brains to determine the difference between 'pluralism' and 'separatism'!

Angela Wood defines pluralism as, "Minority groups participating in a just society: equal rights with the majority; cultural status for all."[5]

I tend to warm to this latter understanding. It is dangerous to conjure up an image of 'ghetto' groups being marked out for racist reasons; indeed, the root of racism is ignorance. I see Angela's definition, with the emphasis on "equal rights with the majority; cultural status for all", as being significant. The danger with separatism is that through separation it becomes more difficult to apply equal rights. Pluralism, however, should have built-in safeguards.

This all seems rather abstract, though; a clear, healthy model of pluralism in operation can be found in the development of 'multicultural education'.

I would suggest that in any 'secular' state school, multicultural education is the only model that will adequately educate children as citizens of tomorrow's world – a world that will undoubtedly be multicultural. I would even advocate the application of multicultural education in largely monocultural areas, since the wider world will increasingly become less monocultural. It should also be closely linked with the delivery of equal opportunities. Schools should become safe environments for all. Schools are 'public' places, where different cultures can merge and share their values – or not as the case may be. Just as a fly is attracted to dirt, so is a bee to honey. We need to learn that certain kinds of behaviour cannot be changed, and safeguards need to be built into 'public' environments to ensure general forms of offence should be removed; where they cannot be avoided then we should be taught how to respond appropriately. Equal opportunities should not aim to make everyone into a dull homogeneous whole. Humans are not like that; we are all different, but we should strive to provide equality of opportunity, to ensure that the rights of individuals and groups are not denied.

Recognising this, in education it would be wrong to allow one religion or ideology to predominate. This is probably my greatest criticism of the ERA as far as RE is concerned. The Act returns RE to the Dark Ages by assuming that this country is 'in the main, Christian' and that RE should reflect this 'fact'. Many of the problems arising as a result of such a stance have been mentioned above. It is interesting to see that the Catholic Commission for Racial Justice has said: "Religions and cultures are closely interwoven and often religion is the very 'soul' of culture." I think they're right. To deny religion is to deny the soul of culture. The heart of the solution for co-existence, therefore, lies in the understanding of culture; in this, RE has thus an important role to play. It saddens me to see something so apparently important being treated as a token subject in schools. Could this be because Mammon is placed before God?

Critics still say that simply having identifiable groups does not guarantee equality of opportunity: "Certainly the mere presence of identifiably different groups within a society is no guarantee of equal participation as citizens, equal life-chances, or equality of opportunity.'[6]

I would contend, though, that pluralism takes us down the road of equality further than any other.

There are various approaches found in religious education. They are:

1. The 'confessional', or dogmatic, approach. This is the assumption that only one way can be right. If two faiths oppose each other – along comes the Spanish Inquisition! The Cardinal's ideas are an example of this method.
2. The anti-dogmatic approach, in which RE is treated as an academic, dispassionate and objective study. This is supported by groups such as the Secular Society. Very good if the coffin lid of RE is to be nailed down even tighter. Usually it encourages pupils to fall asleep during RE lessons!
3. The phenomenological, or undogmatic, approach, which sees the aim of RE as the promotion of understanding and uses the tools of scholarship in order to enter into an emphatic experience of the faith of individuals or groups. It does not seek to promote one religious viewpoint but it recognises that the study of religion must transcend the merely informative.

To sum up, I have outlined three possible approaches to education:

i) Assimilation, a non-starter in my view;
ii) Separatism, which is important and should be allowed and encouraged when the need arises; and
iii) Pluralism, which should be applied to those not encompassed by separatism.

Of course, the argument and study do not stop there. Even within multicultural education several approaches have been used, with some variation between them. Space does not allow me to enter into detailed definitions (which can be found in established educational texts) but I would like to name a few which have been tried: multicultural, multi-ethnic, multiracial, immigrant, poly-ethnic and anti-racist. Most are self-explanatory, but there is one significant point to be made; these models are based on their application in a capitalist society and Islām is not 'capitalist'. Islām will not actively promote Western capitalist values; rather it will denounce them as wasteful, discriminatory and highly-damaging to the well-being of society. Western capitalism promotes greed and unhealthy competition (hence the need for a monopolies commission!).

It is misleading to assume that Islāmic values will happily fit in with those applied in the West. It is rather like petrol and steam engines, both of which work efficiently when finely tuned but work less than well, if at all, when parts of one are fitted to the other. If you don't know how each of these engines works, the result will be chaotic. However, in a strange way, to take the analogy further, these machines behave differently. The petrol engine may be faster and more convenient to use, but it pollutes more and may ultimately bring about more harm than good. So it is with Islām and the Western value-system but I have met very few who, without prejudice, have come to a state of understanding or appreciation of both. Autonomy for both must be allowed.

Muslims will not become British until we redefine the word 'British'. If we mean British in the sense of 'traditional British values' then I would suggest that Muslims are, in fact, closer to those today than the supposedly-British are. The values of family life, honesty and integrity seem to be diminishing in various areas of British society today.

The following words of George Bernard Shaw give plenty of food for thought: "I have always held the religion of Muḥammad in high estimation because of its wonderful vitality. It is the only religion which appears to me to possess that assimilating capacity to the changing phase of existence which can make itself appeal to every age. I have studied him, the wonderful man, and in my opinion far from being an anti-Christ he must be called the Saviour of Humanity. I believe that if a man like him were to assume the dictatorship of the modern world, he would succeed in solving its problems in a way that would bring it much-needed peace and happiness: I have prophesied about the faith of Muḥammad that it would be acceptable to the Europe of tomorrow as it is beginning to be acceptable to the Europe of today."[7]

I would like to conclude with the following:

> *You are the best of peoples evolved for mankind,*
> *enjoining what is right,*
> *forbidding what is wrong,*
> *and believing in Allāh.*
> *If only the People of the Book had faith, it were best for them:*
> *among them are some who have faith,*
> *but most of them are perverted transgressors.*[8]

1. Giddens, 1989 CE, p. 735.
2. Roy Todd, *Education in a Multicultural Society*, p. 38.
3. *Al-Qur'ān*, chapter 4, verse 59.
4. Giddens, 1989 CE, p. 746.
5. Angela Wood, Schools Council, 1984 CE.
6. Roy Todd, *Education in a Multicultural Society*, p. 38.
7. George Bernard Shaw, *The Genuine Islām*.
8. *Al-Qur'ān*, chapter 3, verse 110.

The Case for Muslim Schools

Ibrahim Hewitt

Muslim communities all over the world are engaged in what can best be described as a damage limitation exercise in terms of their children's education. Living in societies largely unfriendly to the Islāmic ethos, they are turning to Muslim schools in order to preserve as best they can their communal identity and practice as Muslims. Schools are springing up in Britain, Australia, South Africa, Ireland, mainland Europe and the USA. At a time when schools in 'Muslim' countries are following the Western educational model in increasing numbers, Muslims in largely but not exclusively English-speaking countries are attempting to revive the spirit of Islāmic education through schools which cover all aspects of the modern syllabus from an Islāmic viewpoint and attempt to give their pupils a solid grounding in their faith through study of the *Qur'ān*, the *Ahādīth*, Islāmic history and the Arabic language.

The degree of opposition to Muslim schools, particularly in Britain, is grossly out of proportion to the scale of the projects concerned. Given that there are, perhaps, 3-400,000 Muslim children of school age in Britain, why should schools which can cater (at the moment) for only around 2% of those children be the cause of so much concern, especially when a third of all schools in England and Wales are religious schools based on the Judeo-Christian faiths?

It is often said that the existence of state-funded religious schools in Britain is an accident of history which bears no relevance to society today, wherein many faiths are represented, not just Christianity and Judaism. Such a view could be taken seriously were it not for the fact that voluntary aided (and some grant-maintained) schools with a religious ethos are increasing in numbers, not remaining static or decreasing. In a democratic society such as ours, then, can it be reasonable to allow state funding for some faiths whilst denying it to others? Should Muslims and other faith groups be expected to pay for Christian and Jewish schools without having similar educational choice for their own children? Critics say that the choice is there; Muslims can have private, fee-paying schools if they want 'separate' education for their children, and this is true. But it doesn't help to explain the anomaly of the funding of some religious schools out of the public purse but not others.

However, Muslims do not want to send their children to Muslim schools – and have those schools legitimately paid for by the state – simply because "the Christians and Jews have such schools so we want them too". Nor are those parents keen on the establishment of Muslim schools 'fundamentalists' who want to deny their children the full and balanced curriculum required by law in the state system. They want them because a *complete* Islāmic education as delivered in a well-resourced Muslim school fulfils the legal requirements for an education which "promotes the spiritual, moral, cultural, mental and physical development of pupils at the school and of society..."[1] in a way which no 'ordinary' state school can do for its Muslim pupils.

However, I used the phrase 'damage limitation exercise' because I believe this best describes what Muslims are trying to do at the moment and it gives an idea of what – despite the ideals aimed for – we can realistically hope to achieve in the present climate of world affairs.

Now, perhaps more than ever before, secularism is sweeping the world in all matters of public life: religion is being relegated more and more to strictly personal beliefs punctuated by occasional symbols of communal practice. Even amongst Muslims, faith does not play the all-embracing role in life that it should, indeed must, if Islām is really going to be an effective means by which society can be run. Historically, it has been seen that occupying forces have sought to introduce changes in local education systems as a means of social control to mould the local population so that the ideology of the rulers becomes dominant. Western nations did this wherever they were the colonial powers, as did the Russian communists after the carve up of Eastern Europe in the aftermath of World War II. The effects of both are still being felt. In Muslim countries, the traditional madrasah system of education was supplanted by 'modern', i.e. secular, Western institutions which grew on the premise that they must be superior simply because they were from the West. Instead of rising to the educational challenge this situation provided, by trying to widen the scope of the madrasahs to include what are now termed 'secular' subjects studied from a solid base steeped in Islāmic knowledge, local populations acquiesced and relegated Islāmic education to an inferior rôle. Such a subservient mentality has survived and exists in Muslim minds to this day.

In Britain this much is obvious, with Muslim parents pushing their children to obtain secular qualifications at the expense of any serious religious knowledge, the latter being entrusted to largely poorly resourced and staffed supplementary schools. Sadly, even this basic Islāmic education is not backed up in many cases by good Islāmic practice in the home. The result is many young Muslims who have little or no knowledge of their supposed faith in terms of the basic beliefs, and no feeling at all that their 'faith' as such can have a vital part to play in every sphere of their lives.

The state education system aids and abets this sorrowful state of affairs by limiting Religious Education (RE) to one lesson per week, dealing with all religions on a relatively superficial level. To be fair, there are many teachers who make great efforts to ensure that all pupils are given the chance to express their beliefs positively within schools but they are swimming against the tide of secularism which makes RE the most marginalised subject on the curriculum. (This is despite the fact that RE is the only subject it has been compulsory to teach in schools since the passing of the 1944 Education Act!)

It is from this position – an education system which largely regards religion as a nuisance best ignored, a society which places religion out of the public sector and a world which is increasingly anti-Islāmic, even anti-religion – that some Muslim parents have felt the need to open schools where their children can be well-versed in their Islāmic heritage while studying for those still-coveted qualifications which will allow them to compete for jobs in the wider community and become the pioneers in all spheres of life and study which that heritage demonstrates Muslims were in the past.

So what is a 'Muslim school'? Is it, as some maintain, a place where the children are given a *Qur'ān* at 8.30 am for it to be taken from them at 3.30 pm; where they sit and chant verses from the Holy Book with no understanding, being beaten if they err; where girls are deprived of equal opportunity and are conditioned for a life of subservience at home; where Islāmic 'fundamentalism' breeds 'fanatics'? Such is the standard and substance of the arguments against Muslim schools. The answer, quite simply, is 'no' on all counts.

Admittedly, there are some parents who send their children, particularly girls, to Muslim schools merely because the law demands that they receive an education until they are 16 years old and they would rather send them to a Muslim school (which at secondary level will not have the distractions of members of the opposite sex) than an ordinary school. Such parents are in the minority though and most people involved in running Muslim schools are dedicated to Islāmic education in its fullest sense.

This dedication means that schools exist where common sense dictates that they should not; in old factories, terraced houses and portacabins, minor educational miracles take place every day. Teachers – not all of them Muslims – deliver a curriculum which does not contravene Islāmic sensitivities in often straitened circumstances, giving the children in their charge a solid base from which to tackle higher education confident in their self-belief as Muslims, unlike their frequently religiously-confused counterparts educated in the state system.

It has been said that "Islām views education as a process through which a child's total personality is developed in preparation for both this life and the *Ākhirah* (life after death)."[2] This gives an insight into the ethos of a Muslim school, in which all aspects of a child's life are catered for, not merely the secular, material side. Practically-speaking, this means that the tenets of Islām influence every part of the curriculum, something not possible in non-Muslim schools. This does not mean that some subjects are avoided if they contradict Islām or entail un-Islāmic practice; the subjects themselves may not be taboo, but the methodology used to teach them in state schools certainly is. Hence, Muslim schools' curricula are tailored to meet the requirements of Islām so that the pupils get the benefit of study without having to compromise on religious principles. Apart from the academic value of this approach, it also boosts the self-esteem of Muslim pupils who are made fully aware of the tremendous contributions made by Muslim scholars in many subject areas (e.g. science, mathematics, geography, etc.) over the centuries.

Another benefit of Muslim schools is not directly linked to the academic side of school affairs but is important nevertheless. The schools do not provide an alien environment, differing in almost every respect from what the children experience at home. Thus, by making pupils feel more at ease at school, they have a positive effect on their outlook and academic achievements. The spirit of the Bullock Report (*A language for life*, 1975), which looked into community languages but could easily be applied in this instance, is encapsulated by the role of Muslim schools in the overall sphere of a child's life: "No child should be expected to cast off the language and culture of the home as he crosses the school threshold, nor live and act as though school and home represents two totally separate, and different, cultures which have to be kept apart."

The criticism that the sheer size (mostly small) of Muslim schools makes it impossible for them to offer a "full and balanced curriculum" is not borne out by reality. Yes, financial resources (or, rather, the lack of them) often impose limits on what can be offered in curriculum terms, but school size in itself is not a barrier to scholastic success. Other, non-Muslim, independent schools (for example, St. Peter's School in Northampton) are small by 'normal' standards (i.e. in official parlance, they are incapable of offering 'a full and balanced curriculum') but are tremendously popular with parents and pupils and are achieving academic results the envy of many much larger schools. There are also many small schools in the state system which resolutely refuse to conform to imposed size limits which dictate their closure and fight to stay open; they are popular with parents and some have received official recognition for the quality of their curriculum delivery. A case in mind is Ennerdale and Kinniside Primary School in north-west England which, with 40 or so pupils, was reported to have received "... the British educational world's most coveted prize: a gold star from Her Majesty's Inspectors."[3] It is, I believe, not insignificant for this discussion to note that Ennerdale and Kinniside Primary is a Church of England school. It is also interesting to note that an independent Roman Catholic school in Wales was given grant-maintained status (state funding) in May 1996 even though it plans to have a maximum of 247 pupils, far less than the standard, generally-accepted norm for secondary schools.

The position of Muslim women, who are regarded as oppressed by many non-Muslims (possibly because of the un-Islāmic behaviour of many Muslim men in this respect), surfaces frequently whenever the Muslim schools issue is raised. However, far from trying to restrict educational opportunities for Muslim girls, Muslim schools actually provide places where they can study and practice their faith, something not always possible in non-Muslim institutions. 'Equal rights' is used frequently as a euphemism for 'do not follow your religion' and I would assert that those who seek to 'liberate' Muslim girls from Islām are themselves placing limits on what they believe Muslim girls practising their religion are capable of achieving. Given the opportunity, any girl can be a fully-practising Muslim *and* a surgeon, solicitor, accountant, engineer or whatever. One lady I know is a wife and mother with six children, all born before she obtained a PhD in mechanical engineering. She is also a practising Muslim in every sense of the word who sees her studies as an aspect of *'Ibādah* (worship). Why should a person's spiritual and religious nature be suppressed for material advancement in the name of 'liberation'?

The sort of problems faced by Muslim girls who wear Islāmic dress are well-recorded because they make good headlines in the newspapers (e.g. the case of the Alvi sisters who were banned from attending Altrincham Grammar School for Girls in 1990 because they insisted on wearing correct Islāmic clothing; and the case of two French girls who were not allowed to wear head scarves in their fanatically secular state school in 1993). However, boys and girls face similar problems relating to dress and personal hygiene which make them ready targets for bullying which, in turn, affects their academic performance. Like many of their contemporaries around the country, some of the girls attending Zakaria School in Yorkshire joined the school from the state system and so, unlike critics of Muslim schools, they are in a position to make comparisons based on experience. One girl has said, "I was taunted about clothes, fell behind in my lessons, dreaded PE [physical education] and worried about school dinners."[4] Such fears do not exist for her at Zakaria.

The fear of intolerance and what has been termed voluntary apartheid prompts many opposed to Muslim schools to claim that children need to be in multi-faith schools which reflect society if they are not to develop intolerant attitudes towards those of other faiths (and no faith). Others propose that schools be made purely secular in nature, in other words religion-free zones, to achieve the same aim. Such arguments fail, not least because secularism is not a neutral position to adopt; those who advocate a secular lifestyle do so out of choice. Why should they be allowed to impose their chosen lifestyle upon others with differing views? This sort of intolerance in the name of tolerance makes a mockery of freedom to choose and, indeed, the law of the land which states that "... so far as is compatible with the provision of efficient instruction ... and the avoidance of unreasonable public expenditure, pupils are to be educated in accordance with the wishes of their parents."[5] The 'multi-faith' argument could be sustained if British, or any, society was truly multi-faith. It is not. Britain's is a society consisting of people with many faiths. The difference is enormous because whilst the former implies that society has many faiths, the latter paints the real picture that people within society only have one faith (or none at all) each. While, therefore, multi-faith schools have everyone celebrating *'Īd* one week, Christmas the next, Passover the week after, and so on, in the real world Muslims celebrate *'Īd*, Christians celebrate Christmas and Jews celebrate Passover. In this respect, religious schools are more a true reflection of a multi-faith society than multi-faith schools. As far as Islām is concerned, it is reasonable to mention here that a deep study of the *Qur'ān* (something which is quite feasible within a Muslim school but almost impossible in a non-Muslim institution) will, as a matter of course, lead to a study of the followers of prophets Jesus and Moses (peace be upon them both) which, in turn, can lead on to a study of modern-day Christianity and Judaism. As for intolerance, a glance at the *Qur'ān* will show that Muslims are urged to "Say ... unto you, your way, unto me mine"[6] and are advised that "There is no compulsion in religion ..."[7]

The public image of Muslim schools needs improvement. The fact that an article such as this is still deemed necessary illustrates that our public relations efforts have been less than successful.

I once had the duty to escort the local Member of Parliament, Ken Livingstone, around Islāmia Primary School and he remarked that he had expected to find a "school for trainee ayatollahs"; instead, he found "a happy, ordinary school" which just happened to have Islām as its ethos. It is a sad fact of life, though, that not everyone has been so positive about the role of Muslim schools in our society; many of the schools' critics would call themselves Muslims but they have failed to see the distinction between their perceptions of Muslim schools, formed by what they read in the media, and reality. The belief in the minds of such people is most definitely that 'West is best' and they are so desperate to prove their Britishness that they take every opportunity to denounce Muslim schools in the press. The newspapers, for their part, exploit this split in the ranks of the Muslim community as part of their own agenda against Islām. They use the word 'separate' liberally when describing Muslim schools,[8] a term rarely, if ever, applied to other religious schools and which is used by those whose aim is to condemn our schools as the products of a narrow-minded, ghetto mentality. The words 'Asian' and 'Muslim' are, in the hands of journalists and commentators, interchangeable, as if they are one and the same,[9] implying that one of the criteria for entry to Muslim schools is race (which is not true); the conclusion drawn is that they must, therefore, be racist and thus undesirable. Such reporting adds to the myth that the schools are Asian ghettos which exclude other races (and faiths) but it conveniently ignores the fact that many state schools in predominantly Asian areas (such as parts of Bradford, Batley, Tower Hamlets, etc.) are, by the very nature of the population they serve, effectively 'Asian ghetto' schools.

Asian/Muslim interchange was graphically illustrated during the dispute at Stratford School in east London, one of the early grant-maintained schools. The details of the case do not need to be mentioned here, suffice to say that one newspaper leader column[10] referred to the "ethnic element" of the school's pupils; the unity of "Asians and Afro-Caribbeans" about the school and that most "Asian parents" support a successful school. This was followed by: "There is, of course, a minority of Muslims who want to see Muslim pupils in Muslim schools taught by Muslim teachers." All along the issue had been about race and one of the main protagonists, a Sikh teacher-governor, had denied that the aim was to have a Muslim school,[11] and yet Muslims and Muslim schools were introduced into the equation totally out of context. This sort of bias in the media is not uncommon. Journalists also tend to ignore the unpalatable truth that if the Jews are definable as a race, then Jewish schools are, quite simply, racist. The fear of being labelled "anti-Semitic" is obviously greater than the desire for balanced reporting. There are some rare exceptions to this but they are still in the minority.

Could it be that the benefits of a full Islāmic education are known to the powers-that-be and this in itself is driving the movement to prevent Muslims from being proactive in the education of their children? Knowledge empowers communities to achieve their potential; does this conflict with 'their' plans for Muslims in this country?

It is extraordinary that opposition to Muslim schools is so widespread: politicians, journalists, teachers and the general public all find the will to abandon their sense of justice and equality in order to deprive the largest non-Christian religious group in Britain of access to equal opportunities given freely to others. In my dealings with authorities and the media in this respect, I have always been at pains to stress the multiracial nature of Islām so it is difficult for me to accuse them in particular of racism behind their opposition. Maybe Islāmophobia, one of those 'new' words, could be used with some justification. With the public, though, it is a different matter: every time I have had a letter published in the national press obscene letters arrive are received and almost all are racist in tone. Despite my name, the pathetic individuals who write to me assume that because I am a Muslim, I must be a non-white; they 'plan' their letters accordingly in a way reminiscent of those 18th century anti-Catholic protesters whom Defoe described as "Stout fellows that would spend the last drop of their blood against Popery that do not know whether it be a man or a horse." Couldn't have put it better myself.

So what can be done? One thing is certain: Muslim schools are not simply going to go away just because the government will not give any financial assistance. Some may close due to a lack of funds but that will only serve to strengthen the resolve of the others, especially in areas in the north of England where there are a few schools relatively close together.

Doubts do exist about whether Muslim schools should apply for what is undeniably their right – voluntary aided, or grant-maintained (GM), status – or whether they should consider what effects such status will have, especially with the requirement to implement the National Curriculum. Aided and GM schools must follow the National Curriculum; independent schools are under no such obligation. Since September 1992 music, drama, art and physical education have been an integral part of the National Curriculum and all, in one way or another, may involve students in work or activities which are un-Islāmic. However, resourceful teachers can and do adapt their lessons to match Islāmic criteria and the National Curriculum Orders, to the satisfaction of Her Majesty's Inspectors, so this should no longer pose a serious problem. Nevertheless, the implications of the National Curriculum for Muslim schools have not been lost on politicians. In January 1992, Angela (now Dame Angela) Rumbold, an ex-education minister, said, "Some of the things that are being taught within the National Curriculum are not necessarily acceptable to the Muslims, for both boys and girls."[12] In other words, she was saying that the mainstream educational system will never be able to adapt fully for the needs of Muslim children as long as the National Curriculum is compulsory. Although the aforementioned resourcefulness has shown Mrs. Rumbold to be wrong to credit the National Curriculum with the inability of state schools to cater adequately for some Muslim pupils, it was startling to hear her admission after years of being told quite forcefully that 'separate' schools are not the answer to our problems and we should send our children into the state system.

It is true that the National Curriculum could be the tip of the iceberg which will eventually sink the aims and objectives of Islāmic education into the blandness that is the monocultural education of today's state schools; and state funding, whilst solving the financial problems of Muslim schools, could well lead to necessary compromise in curriculum terms which effectively negates at least some of the arguments for having the schools in the first place. But some will argue that if our schools can only ever be a damage limitation exercise then such compromises may well be the lesser of two evils; if it is a choice between schools with no funding struggling to offer a decent curriculum and government-financed schools which may have to 'bend' slightly to get and keep their status, then the latter is both acceptable and preferable.

I do not believe that opposition to complete Islāmic education for Muslim children (and anyone else who wants it) from all quarters will melt away overnight if state funding is granted to any Muslim school for the opposition is not based purely on educational grounds. Being part of the state system may well make it easier for those so inclined to ensure that the aims of our schools are not achieved. As Muslims – as a community – we should be more than capable of funding our own schools without depending on cash handouts from the state, and the very existence of our own schools should not depend on government largesse. The safety-net of financial independence if necessary is vital if Muslim schools are to achieve what they have set out to do.

Muslims must realise that although many excuses for opposing Muslim schools are given, there is one word which says more about such opposition than the thousands of words which have been written and spoken against Muslim schools over the past few years. The word is found in a document prepared by the education officers of Kirklees Council in Yorkshire for discussion by the education committee which had to decide whether or not to support the application for government support made by the Zakaria

Muslim Girls' High School in Batley in September 1987; it reads as follows: "More difficult to gauge are the less direct effects and the *ideological* [my emphasis] consequences which would follow the establishment of the Authority's first aided school which has Islām as its ethos." Curiously, when a second, public report was available almost a year later, the tell-tale word 'ideological' had been removed. Caution in this matter persists.

If we believe that the issue of Muslim schools is purely educational we are being more than a little naïve. Underpinning the whole issue is a simple case of *Ḥaqq* (truth) versus *Bātil* (falsehood). The education issues affecting (and afflicting) Muslim children in this country are but manifestations of an international phenomenon which sees Islām cast as the main threat to the 'New World Order'. We cannot afford to be complacent and let events overtake us. The education of our children is crucial for the future of the *Ummah* and every effort must be made to ensure that the education provided for Muslims in Britain matches the seriousness of the task ahead. With *Allāh's* help, it will.

References

1. Education Reform Act 1988, Section 1(2)(a).
2. Ghulam Sarwar, *British Muslims and Schools*, 1994 CE.
3. *The Daily Telegraph*, 27 February 1989 CE.
4. *The Daily Telegraph*, 22 February 1989 CE.
5. 1944 Education Act, Section 76.
6. *Al-Qur'ān*, chapter 109, verse 6.
7. Ibid., chapter 2, verse 256.
8. See, for example, *The Daily Mail*, 8 April 1989 CE; *The Independent*, 30 January 1989 CE.
9. See, for example, *The Guardian*, 8 December 1988 CE; *Ibid.*, 4 January 1989 CE; *Ibid.*, 19 June 1989 CE; *Glasgow Herald*, 13 February 1989 CE.
10. *The Daily Telegraph*, 14 February 1992 CE.
11. *The Independent*, 10 February 1992 CE.
12. *The Times*, 6 January 1992 CE, reporting a BBC Radio interview of 5 January 1992 CE.

The Education of Muslim Women

Ruqaiyyah Waris Maqsood

I am a British Muslim woman who has been involved in education all my life; at present I suppose I am the female equivalent of a *mullah*; I am the Head of Religious Studies at a secondary school for boys (aged 11-16) in the city of Hull. Prior to this, I was Head of Religious Education at a mixed-sex school (for ages 13-18), and before that at a girls-only school. In other words, I have been a teacher all my adult life, choosing what is perhaps the most difficult subject in today's secular society – because in virtually every lesson I have had to 'fight my corner', and have had to take on opposition and resistance from pupils and staff in management positions alike.

To my delight, I have found that the majority of youngsters have actually enjoyed religious education, and many of them have been extremely interested, whether Muslim or otherwise, like young travellers finding water in a desert environment. However, it has all too often been the case that the subject was resisted as being 'a waste of time' in academic and career terms, and therefore intelligent students were frequently channelled away from choosing it into other – more materialistically rewarding – areas of study and all my adult life I have suffered frustration in not being able to do what I really wanted. I have fought, but I have been regularly 'hamstrung'.

All of which has made me very well qualified, I think, to write a few words on the subject of the education of Muslim women.

Women are not the same as men. They have to be stronger, work harder, be more tolerant, more forgiving, more cheerful, more sympathetic. Sometimes they are treated like slaves (usually by those who 'underneath it all' really love them most – their husbands and sons); sometimes they are deprived of all reasonable outlets for self-expression, and sacrifice the whole of their endeavour and effort into loving and caring for the motley assortment of humans *Allāh*, in His infinite wisdom, chose to involve them with. Sometimes we women can choose what our husbands will be like – we rarely get that same satisfaction in choosing our sons! Many of these beloved sons become so spoiled by the available attention and waitress service, that they become absolute 'tartars', and when they marry and become fathers, round we go again. Every woman knows this. Most women put up with it, because in the majority of cases we dearly love our miniature or major 'overlords', and truly want everything for them only for the best – in a way that no other person would.

That is why the Blessed Prophet, who grew to manhood under the care of a Bedouin nursemaid, briefly his own widowed mother, a grandmother, and then presumably a much-loved aunt, gave us the beautiful *aḥādīth* about the importance of Muslim men cherishing their womenfolk, mothers, wives and daughters.

In Western society, this attitude of respect for women is now obliged to come to terms with something little known in many Eastern social groups – female acquaintances not within the family group – the fellow school-mate, female student, female colleague or even boss. Having been part of the student scene for so long, and known so many young men (delightful Muslims, if not all destined to become *mullahs* or *pirs*!), it has been quite obvious to me that it also includes coming to terms with the concept of the 'girl-friend' as a person, and not just as a pretty body to be used.

Liberated

I have had the privilege of being a 'liberated woman' all my life, and have never had to fight for equality either socially or academically, and so throughout my formative years I never really felt the need to be a 'women's libber'. In later life, however, I divorced my first husband after a very long marriage (23 years), and am now blessed with a very happy second marriage, to a very devout and delightful Muslim husband. This has brought me tremendous challenges, and great joy; at the same time, it has opened my eyes to other areas of the world (I knew nothing beyond the land of Palestine before), and to some areas of deep concern to me, both as a woman and as a *Muslimah*.

Once married to a Muslim, I instantly became 'accepted' by most of the local Muslim community in a way that was denied me before (when I had to struggle into the faith more or less on my own). But I also discovered that there was a certain role model into which I was supposed to fit - and which I patently did *not* fit. For example, I have always found the subject of *ḥijāb* rather a difficult one, because I travel to work (in an all-male environment) on a motor-bike. I have been known to rev up the high street in *shalwar-qameez* plus crash helmet, but this is an odd assortment, and I don't think it particularly established my reputation for piety. I cannot help, of course, being English; I cannot help having had a pretty full lifetime behind me. On becoming Muslim, it was accepted that my life had started again – but this is easier said than done.

Some women are naturally quiet, humble, pious, domestic, self-effacing, and so on. I am not. It may, perhaps, be the result of having spent my life virtually in male company that has made me talk, act and think like a man, and to feel totally uncomfortable in an all-female group or society. I can relate to an academic female group for an hour or so; more than that, I cannot do.

I have been devoted to God all my life, and have enjoyed a great deal of travel to various religious shrines of the world – previously Christian, and in the last ten years, Muslim. I have prayed in Al-Quds – in Al-Aqsā Mosque – and the big mosques of Cairo, Lahore, Multan, Istanbul and Amman, gradually learning as I went along. In Jerusalem my prayers were disturbed by men shouting at me because my veil had inadvertently slipped from my arm; in Istanbul I was shouted at because I had innocently sat down to pray in a place reserved for men; in Islamabad I was not allowed in through the glass doors at all (an enormous disappointment) and had to form part of a small motley group of ladies outside. In our local mosque, the *'Īd* prayers are attended by around a dozen women (male full-house, of course), and funds are now being raised for these few ladies to be 'fenced off'. I try to attend *fajr* in *Ramaḍān*, and am the only woman present.

Yet at Al-Ka'bah, that most holy of places in the sight of God, it is made perfectly clear that men and women are equal and may worship together, and that the ladies may show their faces without expecting the weaker brethren to stare at them or give them any trouble or unsought-for distraction.

I have no qualification whatsoever, of course, to criticise what has happened to (some) women in Islām; nevertheless, I have felt increasingly obliged to raise my voice now – even if what I say is wrong, or comes from an improper understanding of Islām.

An Honorary Man

I came to Islām through reason, through the innate love of God, through witnessing so many good things about Islām. It did not occur to me as strange until later that, when travelling about the Middle East as a visiting 'scholar and writer', I was always treated with respect, entertained, fed and blessed with many deep discussions by good Muslim men, many of them 'high up' and notable academics, *whose women were never included* in these activities. In short, I was treated as an honorary man, and never found anything odd in this, as it has been my experience throughout life.

Suddenly, on marriage to a Muslim, it was discovered somehow that I was a woman! Subsequently, a horrendous list of things I *ought* to be doing/believing/not doing/not believing very nearly pulled the carpet right out from under my feet. And this is in *no way a criticism of my husband* or his excellent friends; all are virtuous and kind Muslims, all doing their utmost to follow the path of devotion to *Allāh* as they know and understand it.

It did, however, alert me to the problems of being a Muslim woman that I had not seen before. Which is why I regard education for Muslim women as being absolutely vital.

A woman is more than a man's support team. Certainly, that is one of her functions, and many would say it is her most important function. I agree with that. Many men, whose wives are not very good support teams, must agree with that too. Sadly, no matter how devout and upright, one cannot *force* the correct attitude and behaviour in one's support teams.

The world of education in the West has grappled for a decade or so with the problem of sexism in educational thought and literature. I am a writer. When I write a book, I take enormous care never to use the word 'Man' when I mean 'people' or 'humans'. I have never believed that when God makes His Will clear to people, it is for men only. No honest person, and certainly no honest Muslim, can believe that. If a woman's husband requires her to do something against the principles of Islām, it is her duty to overrule him somehow (with tact, it is hoped).

Types of Schooling

The educational principles of the West (sadly not always fulfilled, but one tries!) require *any* person to be educated to the best possible effect, according to the intelligence, ability, aptitude, etc. *of each individual*, no matter whether male or female. Often this is best achieved in single-sex schools and I think recent research reveals that this old-fashioned notion of keeping young men and women apart while they are studying is not without its justification! This is, however, not the place to argue the merits of single-sex or mixed-sex schools. I have taught in mixed, girls' and boys' schools and personally prefer my current school, which is all boys. (Nevertheless, I have noticed that boys being educated without girls in the class are frequently cruder, more arrogant and bumptious, more ignorant about 'life' and show less respect for women than the boys from the mixed school! There are always pros and cons.)

Girls from a girls-only school are often more lucid, capable of reasoning, more outspoken and more generally clued-up about 'the world' in general with all its problems than those whose education has been distracted by young men. But these young ladies, who have grown up expecting independence, equality, opportunity and so on, are then at a disadvantage when dealing with a society that expects them to 'play the handmaiden' to some man or other. Hence, I do believe, some men are very reluctant to let go of what has been for them a very good thing, a docile, quiet, obedient, domestic help-mate; they do not want to have in 'their' homes a boss, a manager or a high-flying intellectual.

Which is a pity, because *Allāh* in His infinite Wisdom made around 50% of His created humans female of sex and the share-out of brains and talent was roughly equal. Therefore it stands to reason that if men corner all the 'market outlets' for talents, brains, expertise and so on, the corollary must be an awful lot of dissatisfied, frustrated and disgruntled females, with the added danger that they may become resentful and militant and then really upset the apple cart.

None of this can be solved in five minutes. But any Muslim worth his salt realises that there is an enormous volcano brewing up in societies where women's education and welfare is neglected. It is such a tragic waste of resources apart from anything else.

Allowing Women Their Rights Granted By Allāh

The first step must be in the education of Muslim women. In many Eastern societies this has now gone well beyond the first stages, of course, and these countries abound in highly-educated, strong womenfolk who – like their Western sisters – are beginning to question what God-given right various 'inferior' male specimens have to 'keep them in their place'.

An examination of the scriptures is most salutary. It seems that *Allāh* wishes to remind males of the extra burdens placed on females by their biology – they will always have to menstruate, become pregnant, raise children; He is also well aware that women accept naturally the leadership and protection of a good and worthwhile man, especially so when 'love' – that most powerful of all ingredients – is present.

The glory of Islām, as far as a Western woman is concerned, is that it is *not sexist*. The commands and revelations are given to *all* Muslims; their sex does not come into it. This, as everyone knows, was at a time when the West was notorious for mistreating its women and keeping them in subservience. However, has this lesson of equality and equal worth been learned only by the decadent West? A resounding 'No' must come from the female Muslims of the world – for Islām is not to be equated with any particular country or culture, even it originated in the desert sands of Arabia.

Islām does not 'belong' to any group or country or set of believers. It is the nature of humanity to be frequently limited in vision, embarrassed by failure, eager to please and very often *wrong* in what it believes. Humanity cannot help it; it is *not* God. Like the Jain story of the blind men feeling the elephant, when people discover something of God they discover their own bit, not someone else's. When they 'know' something of God, they may be perfectly 'right' in what they know and, at the same time, be 'wrong' – because God is way beyond the limits of human understanding. No person can do more than their best. They cannot be compelled to see what they cannot see, even if what they 'should be' seeing is perfectly obvious to someone else. Fortunately for us, God knows everything, including this, and that is why our *niyyah* (intention) is often more important than our action.

I do not know the percentage, but Muslim females are probably around 50% of the population of the Muslim world. Therefore they are of vital importance and should take upon themselves the responsibility of being just as good examples of Islāmic life and virtue as their men. If they are held back, I presume that on the Great Day of Judgement, a lot of awkward questions will be asked of the men responsible for denying women their fulfilment.

By education, it should be obvious that for a Muslim there are two types for success in life: there is religious education as a Muslim and there is education in the secular sense. Muslim women must take up the same challenge that faced Western women; no-one will 'give' them equality. It cannot be given. It has to be earned. No one can 'give' a man authority or superiority, it has to be earned. The same is true for women.

On the Day when all believing men and women will stand alone and their books are opened before them, it is far too late for whining and recriminations. Every human has the duty and the right to take up the *khilāfah* and *do their best* for the world, their society, their family and themselves.

It is not for any human person to take on the role of Judge; there is only One who sees every action and knows every motive. Luckily, *Allāh* is the Most Compassionate and the Most Kind; and if *Allāh* is kinder than I myself, all things will be taken into consideration. And if the female child will then ask for what sin or crime she was not allowed to live, possibly female children who lived longer and grew to adulthood will also have a few questions to ask!

Education for Muslim women is vital. It may mean very basic education – how to keep clean, nurse the family, learn a simple trade, be responsible for one's household. It may mean accepting the challenge of discovering that *Allāh* has given you a brain ideally suited for becoming an engineer, a nuclear physicist, a poet, a bank manager or a politician. It will not necessarily make the man or woman into a saint. It will not always bring joy and contentment, as every already-educated could tell you. It brings responsibility and challenge.

British Muslims in State Schools: a positive way forward

Muhammad Akram Khan-Cheema

For as long as I can remember there has been an on-going debate within the British Muslim community regarding the best way to overcome the problems of 'de-Islāmisation' of our children. Most of the blame is apportioned to state schools and yet the vast majority of us still send our children to these very schools for their education. I have spent more than 25 years of my professional career within the British education system as a teacher, researcher, adviser and, over the last few years of my employment, as a senior education inspector with a 'quality assurance' brief. Throughout that time I have been keen to understand and determine the needs of Muslim children. My intention *(Niyyah)* has always been to explore effective measures that schools and Local Education Authorities (LEAs) can undertake within the prescribed national and local policy framework in order to provide a balanced education for Muslim children. Muslim parents have always impressed upon me the need to inculcate Islāmic values in the minds of young Muslims.

"What are seen as the corrupting influences of a permissive society are deemed irreconcilable with Islām and it is feared that unless an Islāmic agenda is inserted into the educational curriculum, the younger generation will fall prey to un-Islāmic forces." (Wahhab)

"It is a major anxiety of many Muslim parents that their British born children will move away from their faith, culture and influence." (Sally Tomlinson)

It seems to me that most British Muslims who believe that the dangers of *kufr* (unbelief) are lurking behind everything are actually unwilling to look into their own hearts and minds; everyone else is to blame for the moral depravity of society. There is a complex interweaving of superbly unreasoned argument which allows us to hold on to the high moral ground. The anomalies are seldom explored publicly. It makes joining the 'educators' of our children easy because, after all, 'they' are helping the young to understand their experiences so that they may have a sense of belonging to a community and thus understand shared values and meanings; shared beliefs and insights; and shared agendas and goals. At the same time accusing fingers are pointed at those who provide unsuitable role models, who introduce young British Muslims to a false sense of belonging to and being supported by the community, by introducing them to an anti-Islāmic heritage and traditions. The contradictions in these statements are seldom acknowledged. Perhaps we are all struck by what the Archbishop of York has called the "paralysis of pluralism". We are all so busy bending over backwards to be 'nice' to one another that superficial half-truths pass between parents and teachers. When asked for their feelings on the quality of service provided by their children's school the Muslim parent invariably replies, "I am very pleased with the school; you are doing a very good job; my daughter/son/ward is very happy at the school; the teachers are very good; etc." However, when subsequent, more detailed discussions take place in Punjabi, Urdu or the relevant community language, parents will glance over their shoulder and give vent to their true concerns about the lack of discipline; the reluctance to push children academically; the absence of regular homework, etc. Parents have deeply-felt concerns that their children should be studying essential subjects and passing examinations. They are also worried at the overt suggestion in schools that science is the only paradigm of truth and understanding and that the vitally rich moral and spiritual dimension to the educational development of their children is neglected. Such views, though, are seldom shared with the nice non-Muslim head teacher who is, when all is said and done, doing his or her best. In any case, 'we' are here in 'their' country so what can we expect?

This attitude is bound to encourage complacency and is a recipe for inaction. It is time for open and wide-ranging discussions to take place between British Muslim parents and those who are their partners in the education of their children. I believe that it needs strategic action on the part of influential individuals and organisations, within both the Muslim and non-Muslim communities to break the current unhealthy stalemate. There is enormous scope for progress in areas where there is the most readiness for change. The goodwill exists for a concerted and co-operative effort to address the intergroup conflicts which have thrived on polarisation, prejudice and ignorance.

The Positive Way Forward

In an unapologetically secular society like ours it sometimes appears pointless to argue for a spiritual or religious dimension in educational provision. I believe that the majority of British Muslims feel that the main dangers to society come from those forces which undermine, or threaten to undermine, all theistic principles of life. The pressure of secularism, whether in the seductive form of nationalism or in the doctrines of absolute scientific materialism, and the emphasis on economics as the major priority in life is having an insidious influence on all our lives. The voice of the British Muslim in all this is often a cry in the wilderness; it is either of no consequence at all (as a minority) within the mainstream, or it is effectively marginalised through cultural, structural or procedural means.

There are, however, signs that most faith communities share these concerns and are responding to them in their own ways. It was heartening, for example, to read Cardinal Basil Hume's Presidential address to the 77th North of England Education Conference in January 1991: "It is a matter of building bridges between the rigours and disciplines of academic and technical teaching and the human and spiritual needs of the individual pupils."

Similarly, the Church of England has been a little more outspoken in its interventions in matters of national policy where religious principles clearly matter.

Recent statements by Secretaries of State for Education, and shadow spokespersons, leave the door open for those of us who believe that our own faith offers a great deal more than the secular liberalism which, in educating our children, has failed to inculcate a more positive sense of responsibility towards the society in which they live.

Education and the Muslims

The British Muslim community has shown tolerance and understanding beyond any reasonable expectation over the years on the important matter of the education of their children.

If we examine the situation from the point of view of a Muslim living in Britain today we might say that at the simplest level the two most important concerns are:

1) To make every effort possible to fulfil our duty as Muslim parents in helping our children to be conscious of their heritage and identity as Muslims, whilst taking full advantage of the opportunities available.
2) To ensure that, as Muslims, we are able to contribute towards the maintenance of the highest moral values possible whilst living in a pluralist, predominantly non-Muslim society (without feeling "holier than thou").

Muslims recognise that an education system which is trying to come to terms with the needs of a pluralist society cannot realistically be expected to provide a comprehensive Islāmic education within state schools. It is, however, not impossible to envisage an education system which is in harmony with Islāmic principles. One of the main reasons why Muslims have established a programme of self-help projects ('Supplementary/

Qur'ānic Schools', or *madrasahs*) over the last thirty-five years or so is because the state schools fail to provide an essential part of spiritual and moral education. Other reasons include the absence of Arabic, Urdu and other relevant community languages from the school curriculum; a lack of adequate concern about single sex provision, either as separate schools or within co-educational schools; and an absence of a balanced 'cultural' content in the curriculum.

I feel, however, that Muslims will continue to distrust the state system and will continue to feel frustrated (even if schools try to meet some of these requirements) until they feel that they have a considerable degree of involvement in the decision-making processes and have some control, power or authority over their childrens' educational diet.

Madrasahs are here to stay in order to meet specific needs and give the Muslim community a sense of self-fulfilment. There are grave doubts expressed by almost everyone about the nature of such supplementary provision: the style of teaching, methods of instruction, disciplinary procedures and many other aspects of the current arrangements leave a lot to be desired in most *madrasahs*. It may be said that they meet the needs of ritualistic self-identity and are serving a purpose if only as a form of protest, but one doubts whether the majority of present supplementary schools come anywhere near meeting the spiritual and actual fulfilment of Muslim children. Although there are a few notable exceptions, most parents seem to be dissatisfied with the present provision and consider the *madrasahs* to be far from ideal. However, they also believe that improvements will come with experience, time and better resources. The commitment towards this ideal is unquestionable.

Problems

When facing up to the challenges of everyday life, British Muslims are invariably trapped into talking about their 'problems'. LEAs concentrate on the 'problems' they face in catering for the needs of their Muslim pupils when, more often than not, these 'problems' are associated with the adult Muslim community.

The general image of Islām presented in the media perpetuates negative stereotypes and creates enormous barriers which militate against some of the splendid efforts which have been made towards harmony and mutual appreciation. It also poisons the minds of British Muslims in that it either makes them less assertive or alienates them.

Some of the 'problems' involved in the education of Muslim children in state schools are not unique to them. Many non-Muslim parents, for example, are equally concerned about the influence of a permissive society or the effects of institutional and cultural racism on children who are unable to take full advantage of the education provided without feeling oppressed and harassed. There are mutually-held objections to 'sex education' in the school curriculum because of the subject content or the inappropriate attitude of the teachers (and/or schools) who offer this subject, or the age at which it is offered. Others express concern about the effect of conflicting values and norms expected in school and the home. It is alleged that the standard of discipline and behaviour accepted in schools is falling as is the standard of academic achievement; thus, our schools are 'failing' our children.

Some Muslims suggest that the main reason for all this is the absence of proper Islāmic values; others suggest a variety of different reasons. Most parents, though, remain positively critical; that is, appreciative of, but not wholly satisfied with, the education which their children receive. They have adapted in a utilitarian manner by according importance to education as a means of gaining qualifications and obtaining higher-status employment, whilst maintaining a clear distance from those aspects of British culture which are not held in high esteem, drawing instead upon the resilience and strengths of Islām.

Education for all

In the context of providing an enlightened form of 'good' education within a pluralist society, what the Swann report called *Education for All*, there is an effective and increasingly strongly-held point of view that the changes that have taken place to date are too few and fall far short of the ideal. There is a long way to go before the principles of *Education for All* are accepted by the majority of people in Britain, and even longer before they are implemented and realised throughout the country.

Agreed Syllabuses

Some interpretations of the 1944 Education Act have produced Agreed Syllabuses for Religious Education (RE) that presented Islām and other faiths from a biased perspective. There is a tendency to concentrate, sometimes exclusively, on the outward manifestations of the faith, for example places of worship, prayer rituals, pilgrimage and artefacts, which could serve to deny the deep spiritual values, experiences and meanings behind them.

This, together with the already-distorted image of Islām which is constantly reinforced through the use of over-simplified books written, with the best of intentions no doubt, by non-Muslims (and some Muslims) , and the effects, intentional or otherwise, of secular 'modern' education, *does* influence unsuspecting and impressionable young minds.

Other efforts under the name of 'Multicultural Education' which try to change the ethnocentric (i.e. Eurocentric) curriculum content, promote better intercultural appreciation and celebrate the rich diversity of cultural differences are merely tokenistic. This is either because they simply create another set of stereotypes to replace the old ones, or because they are seen as peripheral to the National Curriculum. They do not change the structures of oppression which are upheld by the institutional inertia built into any form of control, nor do they change the racist attitudes prevalent in our society.

The nature of the discriminatory obstacles placed in the way of establishing voluntary aided Muslim schools is a form of institutional oppression usually defined as 'racism'. There appears to be such a strong 'anti-Muslim' feeling that even Church of England applications for more voluntary aided schools are denied just in case this is used by Muslims as a lever when asking for their own voluntary aided schools. This has meant that members of the Christian community, who should be our allies in such matters, end up wishing us less than well.

The absence of Muslims in positions of responsibility within local and central government either means that we, as a community, are all less able than non-Muslims or that there are discriminatory practices inherent in the 'traditional' institutionalised procedures which prevent equal opportunities reaching us.

Strictly 'Christian' interpretation of Section 26 of the 1944 Education Act stopped the development of Islāmic Studies at examination level for a long time. The first such syllabus received approval for the GCSE examination by the (then) Schools Examinations & Assessment Council (SEAC) in 1990, after an enormous amount of consistent effort by the Muslim Educational Trust on behalf of the Leyton Sixth Form College in London (GCSE Mode 3 Syllabus 3609 Religious Studies – Islām). This was later upgraded to a Mode 2 syllabus (2630), and is now (since 1995) a Mode 1 syllabus (1477) produced by ULEAC. I am amazed at how few schools actually take up this option, and even more amazed at how few Muslim parents approach their children's schools to request that this GCSE course should be offered as part of the RE curriculum. It seems such a pity that our British Muslim children, who could so easily add another GCSE to their record of achievement, are loosing an opportunity. Another good thing about this option is that in their records of achievement this course (1477) will appear as Religious Studies GCSE, and the universities and higher education institutions cannot easily dismiss it as they might if it were entered as Islamic Studies.

There are colleges where teacher training in almost every specialism, including Religious Education (Christian, multifaith or comparative religious studies), is available but only one course (at Newman College in Birmingham) where initial teacher training students are offered Islām as a main subject. There remains a distinct lack of adequate teaching and learning material for the purpose of Islāmic studies.

Superficial contact between schools and the Muslim community fosters some strange and unhappy situations. For instance, in those LEAs where some single-sex schools have been retained after comprehensivisation, a large proportion of the teaching staff could well be inclined towards creating an anti-sexist or feminist ethos in the girls' schools. Muslim parents who often go to great lengths to send their daughters to such institutions will have very different reasons for making their choice. This creates a real dilemma in that the expectations of parents and staff are frequently diametrically opposed to each other. The unintentional consequences of such a situation with real value conflicts put the pupils at great risk, both socially and emotionally. What, may one ask is the purpose of our schools? Is it to serve the needs of parents? Teachers? Or pupils? Parents may be forgiven for thinking that what the head teachers and teachers decide to be the most appropriate curriculum cannot be challenged by them. For many Muslim parents it appears that the education in state-funded schools is imposing a set of moral, spiritual, cultural and social values, not of their choice and certainly not in consultation with them, by those headteachers who have a tendancy to display a fair degree of intellectual arrogance.

The legal rights of Muslims

The Education Reform Act, 1988 (ERA) missed a golden opportunity to offer the same rights to both Muslim and Christian parents. Yet more unintended insensitivity means that, not for the first time, legal rights are denied to British Muslims. The right to establish voluntary aided schools is enshrined in the 1944 Act and yet applications from Muslim schools are seen as problematic. There is a strong, mostly secularist, lobby which has convinced itself that it is just to deny the Muslims their legal right. The arguments against Muslim voluntary aided schools have been well rehearsed; it is said that they could prove potentially harmful to both communities:

1. 'Voluntary apartheid' might go against the interest of the Muslims by 'ghettoising the Muslim community' (NUT 89) thus facilitating discrimination against Muslims in the labour market.
2. It is a threat to "the stability and cohesion of society as a whole". It might provoke a "racist backlash" (Swann, 'Education for All', 1985 and Asian Youth Movement [AYM]). It might exacerbate the very feelings of rejection and of not being accepted as full members of our society which they seek to overcome. (Swann)
3. The presence of Muslims in multiracial schools is needed to help the majority ethnic community to shed their racist tendencies. (Swann)
4. Stubbornness in conforming to the norms and values of the dream world of a multicultural pluralist Britain which may or may not be realised in the next century. (It is claimed that just and rational compromises are shunned by the orthodox/ unreasonable/extremist/ Muslims who have the audacity to demand their legal right in 'OUR' country without wishing to integrate or assimilate.)
5. The best way to meet the needs of the Muslim community is to provide single-sex state comprehensive schools rather than voluntary aided schools.
6. The best way to make progress is to persuade the DFEE and LEAs to develop policies which take account of the needs of a culturally plural society.
7. Existing denominational (ie Christian and Jewish) voluntary aided schools must be encouraged to think of closing down in the name of pluralism and unity within

a culturally diverse society like ours.

8. If Muslim and other voluntary aided schools are established this would deny many of our children the opportunity to share their schooling which is an excellent way to increase mutual respect and understanding.
9. Voluntary aided Muslim Schools will deny Muslim children the opportunities of a broad and balanced curriculum, diminish their life chances, create ghettos, isolate Muslim girls even more than they are at the moment, drop the 'standard' of education, and could create another Northern Ireland situation here.

The logic of this argument

What is forgotten is that most of these 'logical' arguments either assume that British Muslims are incapable of running a school which can provide an enlightened form of education ('Education for All') with a pluralist perspective, or else that, firstly, all LEAs will provide an education which is anti-racist and responsive to the needs of a culturally plural society and, secondly, that all faith communities at present running their own voluntary aided schools will listen to this splendid point of view and close them down in favour of non-denominational, secular state schools. This is the position most of the members of the 'Swann' Committee took but six 'black' members of the Committee signed a note of dissent which I authored. Significantly, it was the only note of dissent in the whole of the 800+ pages of the 'Swann' report.

If and when the education system really responds in an enlightened form, as outlined by Swann, to cultural pluralism there will be no need for 'separate' schools of any sort. It seems obvious to British Muslims today that this emphasis on ideals in the future is being used as an excuse for inaction in the present, as well as an excuse for not considering seriously the legitimate rights of a minority community. The High Court judgement which declared the original refusal by the Secretary of State to grant voluntary aided status to the Islāmia School in Brent to be unsound proves the case.

The result is that the views of the 'majority' (non-Muslims) are forced upon a minority. The perceived needs of this 'minority' could well be realised more constructively if a diversity of 'solutions' and practices were allowed to co-exist; individuals and communities could pursue different objectives without either infringing upon the other's rights or harming the general interest. The DES and LEAs could use their influence to encourage plurality in a setting which ensures equality of access to financial and other resources. Some such choices already exist within the maintained sector – church schools, single-sex schools, 'grammar' schools and grant maintained schools (opting out of LEAs). So why deny a group of parents, pupils, and teachers the right to set up what, in fact, would be community schools run according to their own values and priorities with capital and running costs coming from public funds? Why should such a group be made to feel inexpert, irrelevant or obstructive? Why should such freedom of choice be assumed to be potentially harmful to other people or to the community as a whole?

It is hardly surprising that British Muslims consider the refusal to offer positive assistance for the establishment of voluntary aided Muslim schools (in accordance with the 1944 Education Act) as both unjust and racist.

Such schools would not only provide invaluable experience in tackling the real issues and give LEAs an opportunity to effectively monitor any new initiatives in partnership with the Muslim Community, but would also be seen as a tangible act of recognition of the rights of British Muslims. It would show that despite the power and authority of non-Muslim institutions, the overwhelming desire of a minority faith community can be respected and appreciated because it is their legal right.

"The fallacy of rationalism is the assumption that the social world can be altered by seemingly logical argument." (Fuller)

Good practice

It would be foolish not to appreciate the progress that has been made over the years in many schools; head teachers and teachers have made what can only be described as monumental efforts to learn about, try to understand, show respect for and help the British Muslim children in their charge. Special value must be placed on the contribution that religious education (RE) teachers have made in this respect. Some LEA's can also be proud of their efforts in terms of policy initiatives and Agreed Syllabuses etc. However, those directly involved in such positive developments will be the first to admit that there still remains a great deal to be done in order to clarify the principles of RE, its contribution to inter-cultural understanding, its relationship with moral education and its importance in the broad and balanced curriculum at various stages of educational provision. The ERA muddied the already unclear water concerning 'assemblies' (collective worship) and RE (or Religious Instruction). For some enlightened teachers this has proved to be a blessing in disguise which allows them to interpret the law in creative and imaginative ways in order to serve the educational needs of their children. Such initiatives are not, however, likely to change the misperceptions and misunderstandings that exist in the wider community.

There appears to be a slight move in the right direction in the coverage of this issue by the mass media. Let us hope that those responsible will succeed in creating a balanced view.

Charter for Muslim parents

If there were a charter for the well-being of their children which the majority of Muslim parents in Britain could put their signatures to I suspect it would be addressed to the education system. It would implore those who provide education to continue their efforts to foster understanding:

- by enabling children to become secure in their cultural heritage and faith commitment;
- by offering children a clearly-defined sense of morality and social responsibility;
- by encouraging a positive sense of self-identify, self-confidence, sensitivity, awareness and value orientation which would make children appreciate the need to contribute towards a 'pluralist democracy';
- by exploring the cultural diversity (within and beyond the Muslim community) to enrich children's lives giving a more balanced view of themselves within a multicultural world;
- by widening children's horizons and thereby allowing them to experience a sense of liberation, a sense of joy, a sense of awe, an appreciation of the ultimate and unique gift of life and to exercise the full use of their intellectual skills; without creating a sense of alienation and without feeling a sense of superiority or inferiority in themselves or in others;
- by offering Muslim teachers and educationalists the opportunity to develop a balanced curriculum appropriate for Muslim voluntary aided schools and to share their ideas and experiences within the whole dual mainstream education system;
- by giving the British Muslim community direct involvement in the future development of the type of educational provision best-suited to the needs of their children in a non-Muslim pluralist democracy;
- by offering the right which exists under the 1944 Education Act equitably to all faith communities in Britain: one day this may sow the seeds of trust between the Muslim community and both local and central government. Such a partnership is a vital step if we are to eliminate many of the blockages restraining change.

CONCLUSION

The continuing debate about the educational objectives has not only revealed great divisions of opinion over such matters as the type of schooling (single-sex, denominational, GM, etc.) but also the relative influence of teachers, parents, pupils or other 'experts' and the importance of religious and moral education, etc. At the moment, education decisions are made by the School Curriculum and Assessment Authority (SCAA), the Secretary of State, central and/or local government, school governors and head teachers; in fact, anyone and everyone except the pupils and their parents. Delegation of control through Local Management of Schools (LMS) might give school communities some say about what goes on in schools but that still remains to be seen.

If the powers that be try to meet the special, *but not separate*, needs of our Muslim children and involve Muslim parents more positively in the running of the schools much of the frustration would disappear. Closer links with the supplementary institutions are essential if we are to meet our childrens' needs more realistically. Recruiting, training and re-training Muslim teachers, Muslim cultural liaison officers, Muslim Nursery Nurses, Muslim (bilingual) classroom assistants and Muslim staff within the educational services to take on pastoral and liaison responsibilities should help enormously.

Muslim organisations have shown more than just a passing interest in these developments. The establishment of an Islāmic resource centre could prove invaluable in dismantling the myths and creating an imaginative and constructive means of achieving a harmonious appreciation of Islām and the Muslims as dynamic contributors towards a pluralist Britain. So long as we all, Muslims and non-Muslims alike, think positively about each other I feel sure that we can help *all* children to broaden their horizons and enhance their understanding of a variety of religious beliefs and practices, thus offering them an insight into the diversity of values and concerns of different communities which now form part of our society.

May *Allāh* strengthen our faith, give success to our efforts and guide our children to an enlightened Islāmic life. *Amīn.*

> "Educate your children; they must live in a time different from yours."
> *(Hadīth)*

(This article was written in 1991 and updated prior to publication.)

Educational Opportunties for Muslim Girls in Britain

Nighat Mirza

When an ordinary girl from a subcontinent family enters a mainstream school she moves into an environment that is alien to her. There is a big gap between the system of the home and that of the outside world. It will take a lot of adjustment to understand and adapt to the new surroundings. This will inevitably leave an impression on her mind which will put pressure on her abilities and potential. The first generation who arrived here three decades ago had to struggle physically and cognitively to adjust to this new and strange style of living which was so very different to their cultural traditions and religion. When our parents and grandparents speak of their experiences they show sadness and hurt in their facial expressions; a child of five or six, though, cannot explain *their* feelings. They are left with permanent scars and weighty memories in their subconscious which may have profound effects on their future.

The unfortunate situation we are now in is that a large section of the Muslim community has spent most of its energy in the process of earning basic needs and has not, until relatively recently, thought about or even felt the need to educate their daughters so that they can be equipped for a better future. To facilitate this, not only individual but also collective effort is needed.

However, Muslim parents, instead of providing such educational facilities, have not even encouraged their girls towards that goal. These parents were the victims of the system. They have been caught in the current of the stream; many have drowned while only a few have survived to reach the river bank. It is those survivors who have, due to hard work and the use of intelligence given by *Allāh*, managed to think logically and sensibly in order to fathom the correct path to achieve the desired aim.

Most Muslims in Britain, instead of being determined to encourage and praise their daughters for their achievements, instill a strange fear in their minds. From the time of their first tentative steps outside the home these girls are made to feel that the education they will receive is going to harm them, as if there are unknown factors and forces which they will be unable to comprehend. As a result, the girls feel fearful and afraid and thus dread entering the system. This trepidation does not allow the space and freedom to develop as a strong, appreciative Muslim girl who can look, listen and praise *Allāh* for the beauty and delight which captivates the eye, ear and mind.

The Muslim community in Britain has set up many organisations under political, religious and professional umbrellas. However, there are very few organisations in existence which actually encourage positive thinking and guidance.

Mosques and *madrasahs* are set up in terraced house to give instruction to our youngsters but, sadly, due to a lack of any educational training, few basic resources and a limited knowledge of English (which does not meet with the expectations of children born and brought up in Britain), the teachers' expertise is neither acknowledged nor appreciated by the pupils. There is a practical reinforcement of their inferiority complex and the pupils cannot relate to their teachers and madrasahs when compared with the relatively high standard of the facilities in the state education system. This initiates and catalyses the lack of interest in their Islāmic studies; any learning that does take place under the sorry conditions of most *madrasahs* is often short-lived and is either easily forgotten or is put to that back of the child's mind and regarded as simply not worth remembering.

Such thoughts as these are expressed by young teenage girls when they are provided with an informal atmosphere, frank, open and free discussion can take place. These youngsters ridicule the *madrasah* system and cannot find anything positive to be gained from it.

I feel that Muslim parents, no matter which part of the world they come from, need to move away from a third-world, third-grade mentality and begin to think in a positive, dynamic missionary way that is truly Islāmic. Such parents want to give a good education to their girls using modern methods and tomorrow's technology. They need to provide facilities which are of the highest standard, a pure environment reflecting the Islāmic way of life and teaching staff who are familiar not only with religious knowledge but also politics and world affairs.

The Muslim *Ummah* should make a new start and, instead of creating new issues for themselves, should expend energy, effort and money in an organised manner to obtain moral support and economic help from society at large.

The establishment of a Muslim school on a small scale does not solve the whole problem: from a population of two million Muslims, the fact that a few hundred girls obtain GCSEs or A-levels is not a great achievement. Such results (although individually commendable) are a drop in the ocean and do not even begin to address the task in hand.

In the past, many protests and meetings have been held but still, in the whole country, British Muslims have yet to run just one girls' school to its full potential so that it can serve as an example to all. In Britain it is hard to count even ten Muslim women of whom we can truly be proud for their achievements.

The time has come for Muslims to realise the need to educate girls but the message will take time to sink in: many Muslim parents still only want their daughters to stay at school until the statutory age of 16. However, in the not-too-distant future even GCSE and A-level qualifications will be considered a mere stepping-stones to good education. Is it not possible for a few Muslims in Britain to come forward and give female education the status of *jihād* so that the enormous gap existing at the moment can be bridged? This should be an issue discussed by *Imāms* in all mosques.

For Muslim girls it is essential to have single-sex schools and, more importantly, Muslim schools providing a stable Islāmic ethos if they are to receive a truly good education. Good quality Muslim schools must be established in cities which have a sizeable Muslim community. The building should be of a good enough standard to match those in the mainstream of education; Muslims and non-Muslims alike should be satisfied that the infrastructure of the Muslim schools make it possible for them to provide the best for their pupils.

Parents must be convinced that it is not only a requirement of English law to educate girls but also of Islām itself. Our inspiration should be the saying of Prophet Muḥammad (peace and blessings be upon him): "Seeking knowledge is obligatory upon every Muslim."[1] 'Muslim' in this case refers to both male and female.

We need dedication and determination. Without such commitment it is difficult to achieve first-class facilities. Let us work towards the future of our nation and invest in our children.

In England, most of the Muslim schools (of which there are only a handful, perhaps 44 or so) are in converted accommodation. There are, therefore, immediate limitations on what they can achieve. Despite such limits, though, progress has been made. These prototypes give direction and guidance to other schools so that they can expand, develop and improve on the existing model. By building on this foundation we can accomplish our main aim, that is, to provide the best education for our young girls within the guidelines of Islām. Muslim schools do not offer the dimension of religion alone; they foster strong faith, moral values, a sense of responsibility for the family unit and confidence in individual girls to participate as full and equal members of society.

In such institutions Muslim girls are encouraged to express their religious convictions without fear and they set a positive example. They have given young girls confidence so that by the time they leave school they are good judges of right and wrong, not only on a superficial level but also with a deeper appreciation of life and its aims. There is within Muslim schools and environment where the extension of knowledge makes them aware of and appreciate the existence of *Allāh*.

At the moment, Muslim girls' schools cater only for students up to the age of eighteen. There is a need for single-sex colleges of further and higher education which will provide an environment where ex-pupils of Muslim schools can progress and excel. Parents of pupils who attend Islāmic schools are satisfied with those schools, and the Muslim community is confident that the present position can be improved with additional financial support and further personal involvement of community members.

Muslim schools encourage academic achievement so that students will have solid qualifications to pursue suitable careers and girls have opportunities to study all subject areas in order to broaden their experience. Most Muslim schools have a purpose-built laboratory to cater for science subjects, and it never ceases to amaze that many non-Muslims have reached the conclusion that a Muslim school will be unable to offer science to the students. This is despite the fact that a study of history reveals that Islām has promoted knowledge in all spheres, especially science. *Alḥamdulillāh*, our students tend to do well in this area of the curriculum.

English is important in Muslim schools and is the main language of communication. Students should be encouraged to master the language and study it in depth to examination level. Literature should be taught up to A-level standard. Arabic, French and Urdu can also be taught so that students can communicate well and develop qualities of tolerance and acceptance of diversity. It is great to see positive achievements in these subjects. Students attending Muslim schools come from diverse cultural backgrounds and are multilingual; this enriches the school and strengthens the bond of sisterhood in Islām.

The teaching of Islāmic history in a positive way tries to undo much of the damage done by stereotyped teaching which has in the past depicted Islām as the 'religion of the sword'. Such teaching has left embarrassment and shame on Muslims and so our schools can do much to encourage probing study for a balanced picture of history, thus enhancing self-esteem.

Islām emphasises physical education and in a Muslim school students feel confident and take part in these activities enthusiastically.

With such a broad curriculum to follow our girls have a sense of educational achievement which their mothers share and enjoy with pride.

In spite of all the limitations and hardships, Muslim schools have undoubtedly accomplished much. Their communities praise *Allāh*, *subḥānahu wa ta'alā*, for giving them the strength to initiate this process. Parental involvement is often 100%, unlike in many state schools. This is because the parents identify with the Islāmic ethos of the school and can thus blend into the school environment with ease. They participate in fund-raising functions to raise funds for the school and other worthy causes. This develops the sense of unity that we must care for others as part of a global society.

There are obvious opportunities for exchange visits between Muslim schools and for educational trips to museums and suchlike. Again, parents often give their full support for this; consultation meetings, *'Īd* parties and other Islāmic celebrations serve to strengthen the bonds between home and school.

Although the state schools provide up-to-date technology, without a sense of belonging and peace of mind, active learning cannot take place. Muslim schools provide such an environment and there are fewer pressure on the girls to conform to different standards of 'normality'.

The provision of educational opportunities for Muslim girls is a vitally important issue.

I believe that the Muslim *Ummah* has the means and ability to provide such facilities. May *Allāh* help us to do so and grant us success. *Āmīn*.

REFERENCES

1. *Sunan Ibn Majah* and *Mishkat Al-Masabih*.

Prophet Muḥammad ﷺ said:

If anyone travels on a road in search of knowledge,
Allah will cause him to travel on one of the roads of Paradise.

The angels will lower their wings
in their great pleasure with one who seeks knowledge.

The inhabitants of the Heavens and the Earth
and the fish in the deep waters
will ask forgiveness for the learned man.

The superiority of the learned man over the devout
is like that of the moon, on the night when it is full,
over the rest of the stars.

The learned are the heirs of the Prophets,
and the Prophets leave neither dinar nor dirham,
leaving only knowledge,

and he who takes it takes an abundant portion.

{Sunan Abū Dāwūd}

Publications of the Muslim Educational Trust

1. ***Islām Beliefs & Teachings*** ***£5.00***
   by Ghulam Sarwar
   4th revised edition, reprinted 1996, pp236

2. ***Islām for Younger People*** ***£2.50***
   by Ghulam Sarwar
   2nd edition, reprinted 1995, pp64

3. ***The Children's Book of Ṣalāh*** ***£2.50***
   by Ghulam Sarwar
   3rd edition, reprinted 1996, pp64

4. ***British Muslims & Schools*** ***£2.50***
   by Ghulam Sarwar
   2nd edition, 1994, pp52

5. ***Sex Education: The Muslim Perspective*** ***£2.00***
   by Ghulam Sarwar
   2nd revised edition, 1992, pp40

6. ***What does Islām say about...*** ***£2.00***
   by Ibrahim B. Hewitt
   1st edition, reprinted 1995, pp48

Plus a selection of full-colour posters. A catalogue is available on request.

All prices include postage in the UK.

Please send your orders, with payment, to:

The Muslim Educational Trust
130 Stroud Green Road, London N4 3RZ
Tel: 0171 272 8502 Fax: 0171 281 3457